Team Academy and Entrepreneurship Education

Within Entrepreneurship Education, Team Academy (TA) is seen as an innovative pedagogical model that enhances social connectivity, as well as experiential, student-centred, and team-based learning. It also creates spaces for transformative learning to occur.

This first book of the Routledge Focus on Team Academy book series examines the place and purpose of the TA model in entrepreneurship education and indicates how and why the model has grown in popularity and interest over the last three decades.

This book is aimed at academics, practitioners, and learners engaged in the TA methodology, pedagogy, and model, as well as those interested in the area of entrepreneurial team learning. Readers will be inspired to innovate in their delivery methodologies and to explore learning-by-doing approaches to creating value. This book also aims to challenge the discourse around entrepreneurship and entrepreneurial activities, offering insights, research, stories, and experiences from those learning and working in the TA approach.

Elinor Vettraino is a head coach and programme director of the Business Enterprise Development portfolio at Aston University, UK.

Berrbizne Urzelai is a team coach and a senior lecturer in areas of International Management and Entrepreneurship at the University of the West of England, UK.

Routledge Focus on Team Academy
Series Editors – Berrbizne Urzelai and Elinor Vettraino

Higher Education organizations (HE) operate in an environment that continuously pushes towards innovation by educators. From this perspective, Team Academy is seen as an innovative pedagogical model that enhances social connectivity, as well as experiential, student-centred, and team-based learning. It also creates spaces for transformative learning to occur.

Since its creation in Finland in 1993, the number of institutions adopting this approach has been expanding in many parts of Europe and beyond, and it is increasingly attracting the interest of organizations that want to adopt a model that emphasizes on the transversal competences and skills acquired by its entrepreneurial learners. The aim of this series is to compile the different research, experiences, and stories about the Team Academy phenomenon throughout its worldwide network.

The audience of the books is multidisciplinary, directed to academics and practitioners. Entrepreneurial education and research has traditionally been focused on the individual entrepreneur. However, in the current business scenario, entrepreneurs' teamwork efforts, social capital and networking skills are essential to face the entrepreneurial issues and challenges that they currently face. The books adopt a Team Academy pedagogical approach that focuses on critical factors such as team and experiential learning, leadership, or entrepreneurial mindset, which makes this collection a key information source for those looking at new directions of entrepreneurship education and practice.

Team Academy and Entrepreneurship Education
Edited by Elinor Vettraino and Berrbizne Urzelai

Team Academy in Practice
Edited by Berrbizne Urzelai and Elinor Vettraino

Team Academy: Leadership and Teams
Edited by Elinor Vettraino and Berrbizne Urzelai

Team Academy in Diverse Settings
Edited by Berrbizne Urzelai and Elinor Vettraino

Team Academy and Entrepreneurship Education

Edited by Elinor Vettraino and Berrbizne Urzelai

NEW YORK AND LONDON

First published 2022
by Routledge
605 Third Avenue, New York, NY 10158

and by Routledge
2 Park Square, Milton Park, Abingdon, Oxon, OX14 4RN

Routledge is an imprint of the Taylor & Francis Group, an informa business

Library of Congress Cataloging-in-Publication Data
Names: Vettraino, Elinor, editor. | Urzelai, Berrbizne, editor.
Title: Team academy and entrepreneurship education / edited by
    Dr. Elinor Vettraino and Dr. Berrbizne Urzelai.
Description: New York, NY : Routledge, 2022. | Series: Routledge
    focus on team academy | Includes bibliographical references
    and index.
Identifiers: LCCN 2021040215 (print) | LCCN 2021040216
    (ebook) | ISBN 9780367755911 (hardback) | ISBN
    9780367755935 (paperback) | ISBN 9781003163091 (ebook)
Subjects: LCSH: Entrepreneurship—Study and teaching. | Teams in
    the workplace.
Classification: LCC HB615 .T435 2022 (print) | LCC HB615
    (ebook) | DDC 338/.04071—dc23
LC record available at https://lccn.loc.gov/2021040215
LC ebook record available at https://lccn.loc.gov/2021040216

ISBN: 978-0-367-75591-1 (hbk)
ISBN: 978-0-367-75593-5 (pbk)
ISBN: 978-1-003-16309-1 (ebk)

DOI: 10.4324/9781003163091

Typeset in Times New Roman
by Apex CoVantage, LLC

For Alison, Hanna and Ulla – thank you for kicking me off on my TA travels! And for Peter my beloved, thank you for supporting my continuing journey.

– Elinor Vettraino

For my mother Amelia and my husband Avneet – thank you for nurturing my curiosity, that has always taken me to wonderful spaces.

– Berrbizne Urzelai

Contents

Figures

Tables

Acknowledgements

We would like to thank all of the contributors for their stories, and the learners, researchers, and practitioners for their commitment to exploration and learning by doing. Without them, this book wouldn't have been possible.

Elinor Vettraino and Berrbizne Urzelai

Contributors

Editors

Berrbizne Urzelai
Team Coach and Senior Lecturer, University of West of England, UK
Dr. Berrbizne Urzelai is a team coach and senior lecturer at the University
of the West of England (UWE), Bristol, UK. Her teaching and research
work is on Strategic Management, International Business and Entrepreneurship. She holds an international PhD (Hons) degree in Economics
and Business Management (University of Valencia), an MSc degree in
East Asian Studies (University of Bristol), and an MBA (Mondragon
University). She is also a fellow of HEA. She has experience in working
at different institutions applying TA programmes in different countries.
Her research is related to international business, agglomeration econo-
mies, social capital, and knowledge management, as well as TA-related
country and model comparisons. Her research has received several
awards (best paper 2017 XXVII ACEDE, best doctoral communication 2015 Torrecid, PhD scholarship, etc.). She is a member of different
research groups, GESTOR (Organizational Geostrategy: Clusters and
Competitiveness) at the University of Valencia and BLCC (Bristol Leadership and Change Centre) at UWE. For her publications, see https://
people.uwe.ac.uk/Person/Berrbizne2Urzelai.

Elinor Vettraino
Programme Director and Head Coach, Aston University, UK
Dr. Elinor Vettraino is a head coach and programme director of the Business Enterprise Development portfolio at Aston University, Birming-
ham, UK. She also leads the Aston Business Clinic. She is a founder
and director of Active Imagining, an organizational development and
leadership consultancy. She is also a director of Akatemia UK through
which she runs training for academics, consultants, and practitioners
who are developing a programme of learning based on the principles of

the TA model. Elinor has a DEd Psychology (University of Dundee) and is a principal fellow of HEA and a chartered fellow/chartered manager of CMI. Her research is currently based on understanding how the TA model supports transformational learning for participants and how the application of arts-based pedagogies might support the development of negative capability in team coaches and team entrepreneurs.

Contributors

Isaac Oduro Amoako
Associate Professor of Entrepreneurship, International Centre for Transformational Entrepreneurship (ICTE), Coventry University, UK

Currently, Dr. Isaac Oduro Amoako (PhD) is an associate professor of entrepreneurship, head of teaching, and a project director of International Academy for Transformational Entrepreneurship at the International Centre for Transformational Entrepreneurship (ICTE) at Coventry University in the UK. He is also an associate editor of *Humanities and Social Sciences Communications* journal and a member of the British Academy of Management Special Interest Group (SIG) on Entrepreneurship. Isaac's research interests are in entrepreneurship education, entrepreneurship and small business management, African business and entrepreneurship, social enterprise, diaspora entrepreneurship, and interorganizational trust and social enterprise. Isaac has researched and published high impact outputs and also served as a keynote speaker at prestigious national and international conferences. Prior to his academic career, Isaac was an entrepreneur who started and managed his own businesses for 25 years.

Kwame Oduro Amoako
Head of Department: Communication Studies, Sunyani Technical University, Ghana

Dr. Kwame Oduro AMOAKO has a PhD in Accounting from the University of Canterbury New Zealand. He is an emerging academic with 3 years post-PhD experience in teaching and research. Currently, he is a senior lecturer in Accounting and the Head of Department of Communications Studies at the Sunyani Technical University in Ghana. His area of research includes sustainability reporting, auditing, and entrepreneurship. Although Kwame has an accounting background, he has developed interest in entrepreneurship research, partly due to his experience as a proprietor of a printing press and a small transport business. Kwame has published a number of research articles in the journals abstracted in the Association of Business Schools (ABS) and Australian Business Deans Council (ABDC).

Alison Fletcher
Director and Co-founder of Akatemia CIC UK

Alison Fletcher has a background in education, journalism, media, and technical management and organizational change. She is an exhibitioner at Jesus College, Oxford, and has master's degrees in English and Human Resources Management, postgraduate certificates in education, coaching practice, and coach supervision and is a trained team coach. She edited a newspaper group in Wales, before joining the BBC where she masterminded the transformation of the BBC's archive to digital media management. After leaving the BBC, she set up her own business, The Coach Within Ltd., and in 2011, she co-founded Akatemia CIC, a social enterprise dedicated to championing team and experiential learning.

Chris Jackson
Programme Leader and Head Coach, Bishop Grosseteste University, Lincoln

Following a lifetime running his own successful enterprises, Chris is currently a head coach for the Business (Team Entrepreneurship) degree course at Bishop Grosseteste University, Lincoln. On leaving school, Chris was formally trained as an electrical engineer, moving on to start his own companies, specifically in the field of security and then marine transport in leisure/tourism and scientific survey. Mid-career, he gained a master's degree in entrepreneurship from Durham University Business School and has completed Team Academy International Team Mastery training, developing active networks in the United States, Finland, Romania, Hungary, the Netherlands, Switzerland, and Malta.

Colin Jones
Associate Professor and Senior Academic Developer, University of Southern Queensland

Associate Professor Colin Jones is a senior academic developer at the University of Southern Queensland (USQ). During the last 20 years, Colin has been a strong advocate for innovative approaches to enterprise and entrepreneurship education, and education more generally. The focus of Colin's research is on the development of student agency, transformative learning, signature pedagogies, the scholarship of teaching and learning (SoTL), firm survival, and ecological approaches to social phenomena. Currently, Colin is interested in exploring the limitations placed on learning by the actions of educators.

Sophia Koustas

Assistant Professor, Business Administration and Management, Southern New Hampshire University

Dr. Sophia Koustas has been teaching at Southern New Hampshire University (USA) since 2010. Her experience includes nearly 20 years as a leader, innovator, and connector in various sectors in the United States and abroad. Dr. Koustas has a PhD in Business Administration with a specialization in Industrial Organizational Psychology, an MSc in Organizational Leadership, and a Bachelor of Music in Music Education and International Affairs. Current projects, conference presentations, and research revolve around the development of t.e.a.m. (team-based experiential academic model), experiential education, entrepreneurship education, entrepreneurship ecosystems, sustainability, leadership, IOP, human relations, and culture.

Susan Losapio

Professor, Business Administration and Management, Southern New Hampshire University

Dr. Susan Losapio has been teaching small business management, organizational behaviour, strategic management, and management applications at Southern New Hampshire University since 2001. Along with being a professor and a past co-chair of the Business Administration and Management Department in the School of Business, Losapio has an active management consulting business. Her areas of expertise are presentation skills, organizational effectiveness, leadership coaching, and team development. In January 2012, she earned her PhD in Applied Management and Decision Sciences with a concentration in learning management. She has also mentored many small business owners since 1994.

Gideon Maas

Executive Director of the International Centre for Transformational Entrepreneurship (ICTE), Coventry University, UK

Professor Gideon Maas is the executive director of the International Centre for Transformational Entrepreneurship at Coventry University, UK. Gideon has broad international business and academic experiences. Within the academic environment, Gideon has created various entrepreneurship centres at different universities, developed and implemented undergraduate and postgraduate modules and programmes focusing specifically on enterprise and entrepreneurship. Recently, Gideon has presented various think tanks on the topic of transformational entrepreneurship. Gideon's research focus and experiences are in entrepreneurship, open innovation, growth strategies, entrepreneurial universities, entrepreneurial eco-systems, and family businesses. His research activities are industry and academic related, and he has published various books and articles. Gideon was the past president of the Institute of Small Business and Entrepreneurship (ISBE), an extraordinary professor at the University of Stellenbosch Business School in South Africa, and an adjunct scientific fellow at the Munster University of Applied Sciences, Germany.

Uwe Napiersky
Senior Lecturer, Aston University, UK
Dr. Uwe Napiersky is a renowned business and industrial psychologist. Uwe has a high level of consulting experience, working with complex organizations around the world. He worked more than 20 years in international consulting before joining academia in 2012. As a senior lecturer (associate professor) at Aston University/Aston Business School, working in the Work & Organisation Department, Uwe specialises in individual and team coaching, change management, leader and leadership development, psychometrics, self-leadership, and technology-enhanced learning.

Johannes Partanen
Founder, Tiimiakatemia Global Ltd
Johannes, who is Opetusneuvos (Councillor of Education in English), the founder, and emeritus head-coach of Tiimiakatemia Jyväskylä, currently, is the chairman of Board and the main method developer at Tiimiakatemia Global.

Juha Ruuska
Team Coach, Tiimiakatemia, JAMK, Finland
Juha Ruuska, Phil Lic., a senior lecturer, a senior team coach, has worked as a team coach in Tiimiakatemia Jyväskylä, JAMK University of Applied Sciences, Finland, between 2012 and 2020. Currently, Juha is finalizing an ethnographical dissertation research about its communal learning culture. Currently, he is coaching multidisciplinary teams and conducting research in JAMK's Future Factory. Besides his deep expertise in learning and research methods, Juha has long experience in service design/design thinking, different participatory methods, entrepreneurship, concept development, and leading RDI projects.

Hanna Waldén
Co-founder of Tiimiakatemia Global Ltd
Hanna, a Tiimiakatemia® Master Team coach and a co-founder of Tiimiakatemia Jyväskylä, works as a coach of coaches as well as an active member and a developer of team coaches' network both in Finland and internationally.

Introduction

Team Academy and Entrepreneurship Education

Elinor Vettraino and Berrbizne Urzelai

Team Academy: Philosophy, Pedagogy, and Process

Within entrepreneurship education, Team Academy (TA) is seen as an innovative pedagogical model that enhances social connectivity, as well as experiential (Kolb, 1984; Kayes, 2002), student-centred (Brandes & Ginnis, 1986), and team-based learning (Senge, 1990). It also creates spaces for transformative learning to occur (Mezirow, 2008, 1991, 1997).

"If you really want to see the future of management education, you should see Team Academy." Peter Senge (2008) made this comment over a decade ago about TA, and since its inception in JAMK – the University of Applied Sciences, Jyväskylä, Finland, in the early 1990s, educators and practitioners engaging in TA-based programmes have continuously pushed at the innovation boundaries of more traditional teaching approaches to education.

TA is often referred to as a model of entrepreneurship education. There are certainly tools, techniques, and approaches that are used within the delivery of a TA-based programme that would support the idea of this being a framework or model that can be applied in different contexts. However, TA is a complex concept appearing not just as a model of activity, but as a pedagogical approach to learning and as a process of self-development (personal and professional). As a pedagogical approach, TA draws on the concept of heutagogical learning (Hase & Kenyon, 2001; Blaschke & Hase, 2016) to develop learners' capacity for self-determination in relation, not just to their academic work, but to their entrepreneurial ventures and their personal and professional development.

Since its creation, the number of institutions adopting this approach has been expanding in many parts of Europe and beyond, and it is increasingly attracting the interest of organizations that want to adopt a model that emphasizes the transversal competences and skills acquired by its entrepreneurial learners.

DOI: 10.4324/9781003163091-1

Why This Book Series, and Why Now?

Berrbizne: The idea of publishing a TA book for me started back in 2017 when I began working in the UK, because I could see that there were many differences between how TA was run in Mondragon (Basque Country) and at UWE (UK). In November that year I met with an editor from Routledge and shared some of my ideas which he became excited about. However, it was not until March 2018 that I really started to put some ideas together for the project. I was already in touch with Elinor Vettraino, co-editor of this series, at that time as we were working on several cross-university projects and I remember a conversation I had with her over dinner in Finland in January 2018 (*Timmiakatemia*'s 25th anniversary). Essentially, we were discussing why it was that not many people knew about TA even within our institutions. How could it be possible that we were not using the amazing global network more effectively?

Elinor: In June 2018, the Team Academy UK community had their annual meeting event – the TAUK Gathering. During this connection a number of team coaches met and reflected together about how research could actually inform our team coaching practice, programme design, pedagogical thinking, etc. I was keen to organize a Team Learning Conference where we could invite people from TA but also other EE practitioners and academics to present their work and share their knowledge. At this point, Berrbizne and I realized that we had an opportunity to pool our interests together and publish a book for dissemination as well as organize a conference to share knowledge and practice.

Berrbizne: I was about to go on maternity leave, so I thought . . . this is the moment! I need to do something during this time, so let's work on the book proposal. We created a call for chapters and started reaching out to people from our network to invite them to send us an abstract. The response was great, and we ended up working on a proposal that had too many chapters so Routledge suggested a book series instead. We didn't want to leave people out of this, so we thought *let's do it!*

The rest, as they say, is history!

The Aim of the Series

Surprisingly there is very little published research about the theory and practice behind the TA model, so this book series aims to change that position.

We have four main objectives through this project:

- To challenge the existing discourse around entrepreneurship, entrepreneurial activities, and enterprise education, and act as a provocation to generate new knowledge based on team learning and generating networks of teams.

- To collate research, narratives about practice and the experiences of academics, team coaches, and team entrepreneurs who have worked with and through the TA model of learning, and to offer new insights to those engaged in developing entrepreneurial education.
- To inspire academics and practitioners to innovate in their delivery methodologies and to explore learning-by-doing approaches to creating value.
- To show the diversity of approaches that exist within the TA network (different institutions, countries, designs, etc.).

We wanted to compile the different researches, experiences, and stories about the TA phenomenon throughout its worldwide network. This included not only research but also narrative journeys, reflections, and student voices. This will allow us to get TA on the map when it comes to research as we wanted to show that because you work in TA doesn't mean you can't be a researcher.

There is not a single TA model as different institutions have applied this approach in different ways, so we wanted to celebrate the diversity within the model and to create an international network of practitioners and researchers that work around it. This will not only inform our practice but also offer it externally as something to be explored by other educators that is different from traditional learning and teaching models.

The Story of *Team Academy and Entrepreneurship Education*

In this book, the first of the *Routledge Focus on Team Academy* series, researchers and practitioners explore the pedagogical approach that underpins the TA model and consider critically the way in which the culture, experience, and approach enable rich and deep learning. Key contributions to this text include an exploration of the origins and evolution of the TA model by the founder, Johannes Partanen, in conversation with his long-time colleague, a Master Team coach and a graduate from Tiimiakatemia, Hanna Waldén. The TA model has spread around the globe, with programmes inspired by and based on the Tiimiakatemia philosophy and approach now in existence in 16 different countries across four continents. A founding member of the UK Team Academy community, Alison Fletcher, a director and co-founder of Akatemia, UK, explores the decade-long journey of bringing the TA model to Higher Education establishments in the United Kingdom.

This book presents an exciting opportunity for readers to investigate and connect with an experiential model of collaborative learning that offers an alternative possibility to traditional learning pedagogy.

References

Blaschke, L. M., & Hase, S. (2016). Heutagogy: A holistic framework for creating 21st century self-determined learners. In B. Gros & M. Maina Kinshuk (Eds.), *The future of ubiquitous learning: Learning designs for emerging pedagogies* (pp. 25–40). Springer.

Brandes, D., & Ginnis, P. (1986). *A guide to student centred learning*. Blackwell.

Hase, S., & Kenyon, C. (2001, March 28–30). Moving from andragogy to heutagogy: Implications for VET. In *Proceedings of Research to reality: Putting VET research to work: Australian Vocational Education and Training Research Association (AVETRA)*, Adelaide, SA, AVETRA, Crows Nest, NSW.

Kayes, D. C. (2002). Experiential learning and its critics: Preserving the role of experience in management learning and education. *Academy of Management Learning & Education, 1*(2), 137–149. https://doi.org/10.5465/amle.2002.8509336

Kolb, D. A. (1984). *Experiential learning: Experience as the source of learning and development*. Prentice-Hall, Inc.

Mezirow, J. (1991). *Transformative dimensions of adult learning*. Jossey-Bass.

Mezirow, J. (1997). Transformative learning: Theory to practice. In P. Cranton (Ed.), *Transformative learning in action: Vol. 74. New directions for adult and continuing education* (pp. 5–12). Jossey-Bass.

Mezirow, J. (2008). An overview on transformative learning. *Lifelong Learning*, 40–54.

Senge, P. (1990). *Fifth discipline: The art and practice of the learning organization*. Century.

Senge, P. (2008). *Peter Senge – Team Academy*. Tiimiakatemia Global Ltd, YouTube channel.

1 Team Academy Movement

Its Roots and Evolution

Johannes Partanen and Hanna Waldén

At the time of this writing, the story of Tiimiakatemia will soon reach the age of 30. It started as an experiment with one teacher in his classroom with 24 students. As Johannes Partanen (2020) put it "Tiimiakatemia wasn't created by planning. Instead, it was created with continuous experiments."

During subsequent decades, Tiimiakatemia has evolved into a learning model and a movement that has created team entrepreneurship around the world. Its applications can be seen from primary schools to universities, from small companies to corporations. Wherever there are people doing work and learning together, the ideas of team learning and team entrepreneurship can take place and grow.

The core ideology of Tiimiakatemia is rooted in its Leading Thoughts. They are fundamental beliefs about humanity, communality, creation of something new, and applying ideas to practice. Around this core are the models and tools of learning that hundreds and thousands of team learners use to challenge themselves and each other every day. They have been originally developed at the heart of Finland in Tiimiakatemia. From there, they have spread around the world, at the same time being co- and further developed with hundreds of passionate team advocates who see the power and impact of team learning and team entrepreneurship.

In this chapter, we'll travel to the birthplace of Tiimiakatemia and some of its core development phases. The first part explores Tiimiakatemia from the perspective of innovation. The second part explores the core model of creating team entrepreneurship, The Rocket Model – the roots and core idea of the model. The last part creates an overview of the system of coaching team coaches that is an essential element in rooting and spreading the ideas and learning methods into different communities and cultures.

DOI: 10.4324/9781003163091-2

Tiimiakatemia Is an Innovation

Working with innovations is about the in-born human desire to do history. It is about the yearning to leave a positive mark on the world. The value created by an idea belongs to those who make it a reality, as ideas by themselves and separate from their realization do not have much value. For Johannes Partanen (2020), ideas and innovations are not the same:

> *I've always been enthusiastic about ideas and innovations. However, sometimes I'm irritated by people who do not make a difference between them. Innovation needs enthusiastic people who, as a community, create and use ideas and inventions. Environments that lock up great ideas and surround them with walls are less innovative than open ones.*

Pablo Picasso used to say that inspiration surprises him in the middle of his work. That is why we shouldn't just stand and wait for inspiration and good ideas. We need work that creates space for them.

Good ideas are not born by sitting in your summer cottage in isolation and trying to think big thoughts. Instead, we need connections and networks. And we need lots of ideas to create a singular good one. The secret of creating ideas is about connecting the pieces together with others and with ideas from others.

Resistance is the best way to recognize an idea that is truly worth something. Strangely, no-sayers become valuable promoters of good ideas! Anita Roddick, one of the legendary role models of Tiimiakatemia, created and lived a success story by having an idea about sustainability. She said that none of the business teachings helped her in her business. She was driven by (then) a weird idea and the will to change things for the better.

When looking at good ideas and innovations from the perspective of human history, one can say that our history was transformed by the transition from hunter–gatherer society into agricultural society. Hunters live in small groups that are not strongly connected to each other. In comparison, agriculture created groups of thousands and tens of thousands of people. This allowed good ideas to spread from person to person.

Ideas Develop Slowly

It is a common misconception that an idea is created in a short amount of time. There are, of course, *fast inventions* that get all the publicity. But, most of the ideas are created over long periods of time. An innovation expert, Steven Johnson (2012), calls this process *Slow Hunch*. For example, it took 50 years for Darwin's Theory of Evolution to develop into a new scientific theory. By realizing the slow development of ideas, we can undersign the following motto attributed to Thomas Edison; the ideas that come to fruition are made up of 99% work and 1% inspiration. In other words, it is a long journey.

Not everyone has the material luxury of Darwin to spend his or her time breaking down the walls of known truths. Most of us live in an everyday world where we are constantly under pressure and with loads of responsibilities. Tim Berners-Lee invented The World Wide Web. His *Slow Hunch* took him 10 years to mature. For us, the development of Tiimiakatemia took 25 years. And the development is still continuing!

The New Definition of Innovation

In everyday talk, when people talk about innovations, they actually mean inventions. The focus tends to be on clever thinking, imagination, and creativity. It is all about inventing. But, as Denning and Dunham (2010) propose: what if we are wrong? Could it be that an invention does not bring forth innovation? Would it be possible, that despite a great number of ideas the number of innovations created in the world is small, we are unable to make a difference between invention and innovation?

Denning and Dunham (2010, p. 269) define the concept of innovation in a new way: "innovation is the adoption of new practice in a community." The key to success is adoption. So, if you really want an innovation, not just an invention, you have to focus on the adoption. This rule helps us to create a clear distinction between the two concepts. Invention is about creating ideas, processes, and methods. They become innovative after they are adopted. Innovation by itself is the adoption process!

Part of the innovation is also the idea of community. It encompasses the people who change their ways of working or doing things (practices). How big is this community? The truth is, that most innovations are done in small groups. Tiimiakatemia is an example of this: it has solid learning practices that can be said to be an innovation. The challenge of an innovator is to make people change their practices together and incorporate new ones. People have to be motivated. Resistance must be understood and faced upfront. To get things done and adoption completed, people will also need new skills. All in all, success depends on three factors: domain expertise, social interaction, and recognizing opportunities.

The Practices of Innovation

The current education system does not produce results in the field of innovations. The system is based on a belief that one first needs to have understanding before doing something practical. The assumption is that the students will learn the practice afterwards. We reformers of education try to point out that this process happens the opposite way: one can only gain understanding after doing something. This is the entrepreneurial way. We need more practice in school settings if we want to educate innovative people and be innovative.

Denning and Dunham (2010) present a practical innovation framework that comprises eight practices. We believe that it serves as a good start for transforming schools and companies to become more innovative. And we have to admit that in Tiimiakatemia we have been using all of them unintentionally during its almost 30-year history!

Eight Practices: Reflections on the Development of Tiimiakatemia from Founder Johannes Partanen

The first practice is *sensing*. It can be demonstrated with personal experience. I have been working in the field of education for over 20 years. Back then I started to have suspicions about the way marketing and business management was taught in schools. I felt that it was too theoretical and abstract. When progressive educators started to propose that universities should provide more practical education, I started *sensing*. I began experimenting with ideas that had been maturing in our minds.

It didn't take long for me to move into the second practice of *envisioning*. I started to observe the world around me. Also, I started to read a lot. A new mission of transforming university education to more practical and entrepreneurial ways of working started to form in my thinking. As my process of change went on, I invented and built a story about a fantastic *Trip Around the World*. The idea of this story was simple: by working and studying hard, we can have an around-the-world trip that most people only dream of. I published a Manifest and enough students, a full classroom, joined in. Together we formed a community around this story, and this became *Our Story*.

The third practice – *offering* – provided more depth and understanding to the story. Creating and offering for us was manifested as steps that we needed to take to do the *Trip Around the World*. The previous practices helped us to do that: we had discussions on the Manifest: do you want to travel around the world and learn some marketing while doing that? It catalysed our thinking and empowered us. This practical, open proposal provided us a roadmap on how to get from here to there. And it gave us clues on how to avoid pitfalls on the way.

To move from thinking and planning, we needed *adoption*. That is the fourth practice. Adoption of an idea is easier if one has a roadmap or a model that shows the way the community has to travel. At the same time, people create their shared language that helps everyone to understand each other. Also, to have adoption, one needs allies as there sure will be those who oppose the new idea. I was fortunate to have my own company that already had a wide business network. It provided us support in the beginning.

To keep the adoption process going forward, one needs to have a demonstration project that can show others that the idea is credible and that it can create results. These projects provide evidence. In the case of Tiimiakatemia, we had three big projects:

- The first one, The City of Human Smile (fin. Ihmiskasvoinen kaupunki) was done in cooperation with Jyväskylä Congress to improve customer service in a wide variety of local companies. It ran for three years. During that time, the City of Jyväskylä had its own pedestrian street that functioned as the high street of the city.
- We negotiated with the city officials and Tiimiakatemia became the main marketing developer of the street's marketing. Thus, the second project was named as Development of Pedestrian Street of City of Jyväskylä. Our teampreneurs worked a lot on that!
- The third project was Neste Rally Finland. Then (and also now) legendary rally driver Simo Lampinen wanted to use the pedestrian street as part of the rally carnival. It became one of the biggest event management projects of Tiimiakatemia at that time.

We got publicity for all of these projects. We gained confidence. We demonstrated to ourselves and everyone else that our idea was good, and it could create positive outcomes in terms of learning marketing in practice and benefiting the local business community.

The fifth practice is *sustaining*. After adoption, one needs to make the innovation sustainable and *stick to the culture*. This phase is extremely challenging to innovate as in most cases people have to face all kinds of setbacks. To push through this phase, one should focus on four areas: (1) integrate the practice into the operating environment; (2) make it possible for people to use the practice; (3) support the practice; and (4) face and deal with the resistance that the practice will eventually face.

During the sustaining phase, Tiimiakatemia was (and Tiimiakatemia by Jyväskylä University of Applied Sciences still is) part of formal education institution. We needed to create a curriculum that was suitable for the project and team learning. I spent hundreds of hours creating it. To create a flexible curriculum wasn't easy as we had to take into account both the university's and business world's needs. Eventually, we succeeded in creating a good curriculum. This helped us to deal with the resistance of those who claimed that our approach wasn't suitable for university education. Retrospectively thinking, I reckon back then we created many small inventions that we incorporated into our daily lives and the curriculum as well. For example, I created the concept of the *Reading Programme* and invented *The Book Points of Tiimiakatemia*.

The sixth practice is *executing*. The innovator has to earn the trust of others. He or she needs to be connected to a wide variety of networks. The members of these networks will only trust you if you can produce results. To Tiimiakatemia, our final, concrete result was our first *Around the World Trip*. We did it with the *Round the World Team* (that was the team's name). With the trust and self-confidence we got from that, we were able to get our own facilities and build solid permanent team learning practices.

Sustainable innovations need leadership and because of that, the seventh practice is leading. According to Chinese philosopher Lao Tzu, a leader is best when people barely know he exists. In other words, when great things happen, the team will say *we did it ourselves*. Once a group of professors was visiting Tiimiakatemia. They asked the teampreneurs who is the manager of the place. The teampreneurs said that they are all the managers! However, the teampreneurs did introduce me to the professors later on as an ordinary team coach. But, I felt happy: we had a great leadership culture in Tiimiakatemia.

Denning and Dunham (2010) end their list of innovation practices with the last one: *embodying*. The innovator has to create an open and welcoming culture. Everyone must sense good energies and accept each other's ways of working. It requires emotional intelligence, even good body language. This practice continues even today.

Innovations can be seen as movements. They are about change. The innovators – and the whole community – have gone through the phases previously described, but there is one more additional phase: extending the reach of the innovation and helping others in innovating more! Tiimiakatemia did this by helping Proakatemia, a Tiimiakatemia influenced university programme, to develop in its first stages. Since then, many other *Academies* have been supported the same way.

Mastery is a journey, not a destination. Denning and Dunham's (2010) process is true in the context of Tiimiakatemia! We can be masters by starting the journey from ourselves and helping others to adopt innovations they feel are helpful to them. The eight innovation practices are yours as a team coach, educator, entrepreneur, or manager.

The Rocket Model Is a Framework for Start-Up Entrepreneurship

Innovators need to create new ideas and experiences together with customers and partners. In Tiimiakatemia, we invite our customers and partners to this co-creation process. An open innovation speeds up and deepens the process of creating new services. To have co-creation, an innovative community needs to have a framework. For Tiimiakatemia, The Rocket Model, as presented by Johannes Partanen (2012), can be seen as a framework. It describes the creation process of team entrepreneurship in process form. As team learning is process learning, The Rocket Model essentially highlights this aspect of a process. Models, such as The Rocket Model, help us also to understand our reality and develop our practices.

The Rocket Model was born through a gradual process that lasted 10 years. Its first prototypes were actually just a collection of ideas scribbled on a notebook of the founder. Then, all of them fell into their own places and formed a bigger picture. At first, The Rocket Model had only one process (the team coaching process of the present model). It was followed by a crystalline model of eight processes, consisting of four internal and four external processes. It also had several horizontal fishbone models. Until one day, when the model was turned around into vertical position and The Rocket Model was born.

When we examine the current The Rocket Model as a whole, we notice that it is made up of five vertical *lanes*, four horizontal levels, and 14 processes. Team companies develop upward from the bottom. The foundation level is made up of three learning processes: The Process of Individual/Teampreneur Learning (Y1), The Process of Team Learning (Y2), and The Process of Team-Company Learning (Y3). These three processes form the "engines" of The Rocket (Figure 1.1).

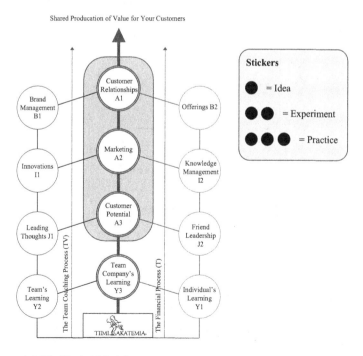

Figure 1.1 The Rocket Model.

Source: Partanen (2012).

The basic descriptions of the individual processes of The Rocket Model are always similar. The core of the process is adapted from the matrix designed by Ikujiro Nonaka and Hirotaka Takeuchi (1995). Figure 1.2 shows the adaptation of this matrix. The two squares on the left describe the Teampreneur's or the team's tacit, or invisible knowledge. The two squares on the right describe their explicit knowledge, which is documented in written form. The two upper squares are dialogic: new thoughts and viewpoints are found through discussions and sharing experiments. The two lower squares represent learning by doing. Alternative theories and solutions are transferred into practical experiments. The individual is at the core, depicted by a little circular arrow in the centre of the windows.

There are three circles around each process (see Figure 1.2). They resemble an image that one gets by throwing a stone into a calm lake. The first wave is the innermost circle. It is always the viewpoint of the Teampreneur's

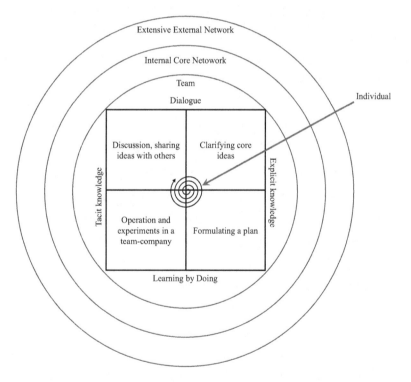

Figure 1.2 The structure of The Rocket Model's process window and process circles.

Source: Partanen (2012).

own team-company. The second wave is the viewpoint of Tiimiakatemia as a whole (the entire team organization), which comprises several team companies. The third wave is the whole network – the Tiimiakatemia Global Learning Network. With the tools and methods of the processes of The Rocket Model, a business can be started from scratch, even without a business idea. Business ideas spring up gradually during the systematic process with the educated team coach.

Coaching Team Coaches and Advancing the Tiimiakatemia Movement

Team coaches must challenge the learning process and create new traditions by giving room for different learning paths, tasks, interests, and ways of working. They must constantly encourage independent thinking. They put the learner in the centre and at the same time put themselves aside to support and inspire the learner and the team to take full responsibility for the learning process (Partanen, 2014). It doesn't mean leaving the learners alone but helping them from different positions.

One viewpoint can be for the team coach to awaken the learners' dreams. Why are some people able to reach even unbelievable dreams, while most people seem unable to achieve even the smallest and the most mundane dreams? At school, we don't learn to use all our true talents. Many creative people have been frustrated with this treadmill and have never found their *own* field.

To create a learning system and culture the same or similar to Tiimiakatemia, one needs to have team coaches. They are persons who cherish the ideology of team learning, can use the fundamental tools of Tiimiakatemia, and have the know-how to build team learning processes. The Rocket Model acts as a good foundation for training team coaches as it includes themes of Team Learning (Y1, Y2 and Y3), Leadership (J1 and J2), Customers (A3, A2 and A1), Innovation (I1 and I2), Brands and Offering (B1 and B2) as well as the special theme of Creating Team Coach's Character. At the centre is a well-coached team coach. To attain a basic level of competency, the learning process needs to be long enough as the learning demands time for adoption and experiments.

In a coach-the-coach programme, the participants learn with each other. They support each other. Tiimiakatemia's team coaching system provides these peer learning opportunities in the form of coaching programmes. In each of these programmes, the participants form their own learning team of 20 to 24 people. During the programme, they strive toward both their common goal of becoming better team coaches and their individual learning goals. Between contact sessions, everyone learns in practice: they apply

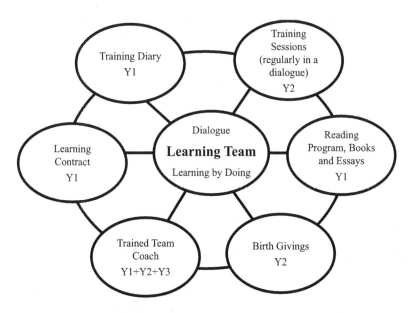

Figure 1.3 Tiimiakatemia small cardinals.
Source: Partanen (2012).

ideas gained from the programme to their own *academies* that vary from single classroom to major schools or company departments.

To provide the participants with a solid understanding of Tiimiakatemia's learning tools, the coach-the-coach programme includes a model called Tiimiakatemia Small Cardinals (see Figure 1.3). It emphasizes the importance of dialogue and learning-by-doing and includes the fundamental tools of team learning. These are, in a sense, the minimal set of learning tools one needs to use in order to do team coaching effectively in the long run. The tools are interdependent and reliant on each other – missing even one may hinder team learning a lot. At the centre of the Small Cardinal Model, there are two central tools: the learning team (of 12 to 24 persons) and dialogue. Around them are the other tools: learning diary, learning contract, reading programme and book essays, continuous training sessions in a dialogue and knowledge creation sessions. And, as a tool, a trained team coach is also included in it.

The growth of becoming a team coach is both transformation of one's identity and gaining know-how on how to use Tiimiakatemia's tools and run its processes. Also, every team coach is a team learner: the team coach identity has the idea of continuous development as a professional and an educator. Team coaches have to jump into the unknown and break their own mental barriers. Growing the *courage muscle* is an everlasting learning activity of all team coaches.

The team creates its own culture, which reflects the culture accepted in the whole organization. Culture is never complete. A team's purpose always starts with its customers and their needs. Every team clarifies who their customers are and what benefits they can accomplish for them. At Tiimi-akatemia, we make sure everyone maintains this customer-led-mentality.

The process is more important than individual results at Tiimiakatemia. We have formulated the following principles for team coaches: 1) achieving results – concentrating on key results, 2) the big picture, 3) finding strengths and focusing on them, 4) trust, and 5) positive thinking.

The Movement Continues

The work with and for the Tiimiakatemia network and movement continues. During these last three decades, the Tiimiakatemia network has grown to be a multicentred, cross-connected, and fast-growing learning network. It has a strong core connected to shared values and core principles and upon those an open flow of ideas and development processes that take place around the network in and across different *team learning hubs*. Complexity and diversity have increased in proportion to the size of the network. At the same time, the number of new ideas and inventions has been seen to increase and the pace of development to accelerate. Networks can be seen as massive teams, the same learning and development principles and processes take place in both teams and networks. By nurturing the core principles of team learning, we nurture the core principles of our shared learning network.

Passionately and with day-to-day persistent and action-rooted work, we ourselves also want to do our best to act as an example of lifelong team learners and cherish and support the work of all the team learners – team entrepreneurs and team coaches – around the globe. We challenge ourselves continually to find new insights and ideas on how to experiment bravely and learn from everything we do. Not by ourselves but with all the hundreds and thousands of co-learners and co-inventors around Tiimiakatemia Global Learning Network. This is the journey we have chosen, and this is the journey we want to continue travelling on towards the future.

References

Denning, P. J., & Dunham, R. (2010). *The innovator's way: Essential practices for successful innovation*. Massachusetts Institute of Technology Press.

Johnson, S. (2012). *Where good ideas come from: The natural history of innovation* (Illustrated ed.). Riverhead Books.

Nonaka, I., & Takeuchi, H. (1995). *The knowledge-creating company: How Japanese companies create the dynamics of innovation.* Oxford University Press, New York.

Partanen, J. (2012). *The team coach's best tools* (original work: Tiimivalmentajan parhaat työkalut 2012, translated by Aki Myyrä). Partus, Jyväskylä.

Partanen, J. (2014). *Glimpses of individual learning: What team coaches need to know about individual learning and the practices of Tiimiakatemia* (original work: Välähdyksiä yksilön oppimisesta 2014, translated by Aki Myyrä). Partus, Jyväskylä.

Partanen, J. (2020, May 19). Personal conversation with Master Team Coach and co-author, Hanna Waldén. Jyväskylä, Finland.

2 Tiimiakatemia Learning Culture

Design-Ethnographical Findings From Tiimiakatemia

Juha Ruuska

Introduction

In this chapter, I will introduce design-ethnographical findings of Tiimi-akatemia learning culture. These findings are represented through four contexts: 1) Learner (individual), 2) Team, 3) Communal (Organizational), and 4) Team Coaching. I will concentrate especially on findings on Learner personas/identity and Team identity.

From the learners' point of view, I introduce six different and diverse learning personas based on the research material. I also introduce a team identity map that shows Tiimiakatemia learning culture produces itself as a community of similar and diverse beginners, who construct themselves towards multiple identities, including entrepreneurship.

This chapter is based on ongoing doctoral research that started in 2016.

I started my *career* as a team coach (senior lecturer) on 5 August 2012. After visiting Tiimiakatemia[1] in 2009, I found out it was different, and also fitted my thinking of how learning should be – real learning-by-doing. Students set up their own (team) company in the first weeks of their studies and were doing *their own thing* – business with real companies.

During my visit, I noticed that learners seemed to have a special ownership of the space – as it was their dedicated *office* as *team entrepreneurs;* not just a public study space that *belonged* to nobody or culturally *belonged* to the faculty. Later, I found out that the cooperatives paid rent for their office space, in order to create an authentic environment for entrepreneurship. The team coaches had their *corner* in the same open-space office as the student cooperatives (open offices became popular in the 1990s), but they did not necessarily act as if they were *in charge* of the unit.

The practice of *coaching* is historically linked to the *Human Potential Movement* (roots in 1960s counter culture), powered by humanistic psychology and especially Maslow's idea of self-actualization (the concept was originally introduced by Kurt Goldstein in 1934). In humanistic psychology,

DOI: 10.4324/9781003163091-3

the belief towards a human need for self-actualization and creativity is central, as is the belief of hidden potential in every individual. Through development, we could achieve the quality of life, happiness, and fulfilment. In humanistic psychology, people are encouraged to open self-reflection, and this is also a foundation for its therapeutic practices. In the 1990s, the practice of coaching was divided into two: 1) Executive coaching and 2) Life Coaching (Grogan, 2013; Maslow, 1943).

The emergence of a *coach* and the practice of team coaching (not teaching) in Tiimiakatemia was an import from business (executive coaching) to the educational field. The founder Johannes Partanen was still a very active reader, and the ideas of learning organization, team learning, and especially the practice of dialogue training with a team coach emerged from Johannes' idea of putting the classroom desks in a circle and eventually getting rid of the desks (Partanen, 2012, p. 8; Ruuska, 2013; Isaacs, 1999; Katzenbach & Smith, 1993; Senge, 1990). In the interview of Johannes, it became clear that he was after a kind of *akido* principle (or the metaphor of *thin red line*) that flipped the teacher's traditional social role and became student (or team)-centred. The team coach, who followed the *akido principle,* did not intervene in the learners' process, but more like channelled the energy to a new direction, where the potential of the learners would flourish (Coach interview 1).

The learners' process is set up as a team process (of 15–20 members/ team). This leads to an idea and a practice of team coaching, where the team coaches the team (company) development process lasting 2.5–3.5 years,[2] not single courses in a degree program. This means that most of the coach's contact hours are spent in the team training sessions, repeated twice a week, 4 hours at a time.

Identity construction is a central theoretical concept in this article. Shaping identity is work that a person (or subject) does with other people (subjects) (parents, teachers, friends, and close-ones). Identity is a creation, just like the work of art is a creation of creative practices. But unlike a work of art, identities are not complete or closed – they are always open for new interpretations and they are never complete – they can change and are changing in spite of their partial stability. Identities are just as much actions and processes as they are products, productions, and creations. This concerns subject's individual or internal forms and group,[3] social or collective identities. Identity work is a process, where social and cultural practices shape subjects in various learning processes. In these processes, subjects achieve different competencies, and at the same time, the spirit and the body are recorded with individual traces of the experiences. Learning is in relation to all the worlds (spheres/architectures) in which we participate: nature, society, symbols, and all ourselves. We learn facts such as ways of thinking, norms, models, relations, genre rules and symbolization, expression, and reflexivity (Fornäs, 1995, p. 281). Identity work is production only in the broad sense of the word: it is not strategic or goal-oriented work, but a creative, communicative practice. Only death ends humans' identity work.

In this chapter, I will introduce ethnographical findings of Tiimiakatemia learning culture. The findings are represented through four contexts: 1) Learner (individual), 2) Team, 3) Communal (Organizational), and 4) Team Coaching. I will concentrate especially on findings on Learner personas/identity and Team identity.

Research Design

Somewhere in 2016, my interest in conducting a cross-disciplinary,[4] ethnographic research or in other words, *thick description* of Tiimiakatemia learning culture (see Geertz, 1973; Van Maanen, 2011), started from the insight that I didn't well-enough understand the learner-teampreneurs' (students) *world* (emic). More so, I didn't understand how and why they progress and (really) learn. It also came to me that there was not much academic research made on Tiimiakatemia, and this would be a tale (as Van Maanen, 2011 describes ethnographic writing) worth telling. In the Tiimiakatemia community, I was an insider (emic), but as a team coach, I was socially an outsider among young adult learners (etic). In terms of professional identity, my multi-disciplinary background and the multi-disciplinary research design (contemporary culture, education, service design, and business economics/entrepreneurship) have eventually helped me to stay neutral and critical enough to culturally position myself in this research. This is of course a claim that's validity must be evaluated in the writing.

The findings presented in this chapter are based on research material that has been collected during 2016–2020, some material was also collected between 2012 and 2015 before making the first research plan of my doctoral research, which is being finalized as I'm writing this. The research material consists of in-depth qualitative interviews of alumni-learners[5] (N=14), learner reflective narratives of graduating learners (N=22), coach interviews (N=3), field notes 2016–2020 ($\approx$600–800), training diaries 2012–2016, research diary, video material, and different documents and learning documents (learner reflections and essays).

Tiimiakatemia Communal Learning Culture

You may see Tiimiakatemia *annual clock* in Figure 2.1, a reduced representation of Tiimiakatemia' s communal level learning culture, especially the learning practices that are shared at the community level and help to co-create knowledge between learners and teams.

Figure 2.1 helps you to understand Tiimiakatemia as a communal learning culture, if you don't think of it as a traditional school, but as a school that aims to construct itself as a community or organization. It is a special kind of organization, as the majority of the 70–120[6] learners are beginners (excluding 5–8 coaches) – not-yet professionals.

The dual-role learners[7] are called *team entrepreneurs* and are expected to come to work (not study)[8] every morning and create team rules, practices, goals, and vision for the team (company) (Field Note, 2017a). This is a lot to handle for a *penguin* team (first-year), with a lot of diversity and with no experience in teamwork and business. Communal learning practices, such as weekly open forums, cross-fertilization,[9] and especially informal[10] and formal[11] communal events help learners to adopt the (learning) culture.

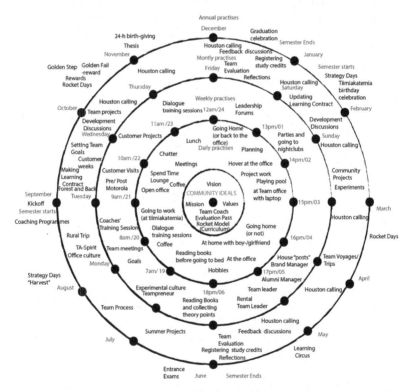

Figure 2.1 Annual clock of Tiimiakatemia – representation of communal learning practices.

Source: Author's own.

There are also practices that aim to develop and lead Tiimiakatemia as an organizational community, such as manifested leading thoughts[12] and *house posts*.[13] This is where team coaches and the head coach (lecturers) play a vital role in facilitating, managing, and coordinating learners' recruitment and dialogue.

The team coaches possess the administrative/institutional power to receive, evaluate, and register learners' formal learning results (study credits) and create the practices for formal/institutional learning, which eventually acts as a basis for receiving a business bachelor's degree/degree programme in entrepreneurship development. The formal evaluation and credits received are based on individual experiential learning – evidence in practice (projects/doing) and theory (book/theory) points/essays. The individuals set their goals freely using a learning tool called *learning contract* (see Cunningham, 1999), with basically no restrictions from the curriculum. Team (company) development is also evaluated using *rocket model*, which has no *formal* status in the evaluation system.

A descriptive example of an *informal formal* or a playful[14] communal learning culture is the 24-hour birth-giving event (see Figure 2.2), where

Figure 2.2 The 24-hour birth-giving event on 14–15 November 2016, event theme "Ancient Rome."

Source: Author's own.

graduating teams (4th year) *give birth* to a business challenge presented by an external company. The event is organized by the community. It can be interpreted as an initiation and/or maturity ritual of team graduation that includes a test: the team has to solve a real business (given by an external company) challenge in 24 hours (Field Note, 2017b; Ruuska, 2021.)

Team Identity: From Honeymoon to Crisis

Team identity is constructed and produced through common, repeated, and given communicative practices, especially team dialogue training sessions, weekly team and project meetings, leadership/social roles,[15] dedicated office space, community events, informal team/community events, and team coaching. These practices support that team identity and culture are constructed, as are common learning practices that all the teams share (see Figure 2.3).

One point of view is normative – what are the rules of inclusion and exclusion (or team identification) in Tiimiakatemia Jyväskylä teams? What is ideal in the team culture and what is disapproved? Some of the norms/requirements are more stable (university curricula) but teams also actively form their own norms (which often resemble each other) and are encouraged to lead themselves as an independent organization.

After the team formation event/phase, the team structure (or the team organization) is formalized through co-creation of a name, establishing a legalized cooperative. This is a concrete act of constructing team ownership

Figure 2.3 Team dialogue training session.
Source: Author's own.

of the venture (independent of university). Through this, it becomes more *real* for all signed up, as before studying might have been a mere *simulation of life*. The construction of *real* is then transferred to *real* projects with *real* customers producing *real* money. This signifies the identity of a *business maker (self)* as a distinction to *student (the other)*.[16] As the opposite, some learners experience they are *students*, suggesting identification to a more common student culture (Learner Interview, 2018a). Yet, most learners see Tiimiakatemia as *a bubble* or a *safe haven*, a transitional place, not as a venture of life and death (of the enterprise) (Field Note, 2019).

The attempt to describe team identity production in Tiimiakatemia is challenging, as at the surface, it is tempting to see all the teams as similar or different from each other. This would lead to conceptualization that Tiimiakatemia teams are *similar* or *diverse beginners*. Still, the research material (Learner Interview, 2018a, 2018b, 2019a, 2019b; Learner Narratives 1–22) supports the description that the teams are both *diverse and similar beginners*. Through learner personas presented in the next section, we can start seeing types of identities or different positions inside the teams/community. This makes it also possible to present the team identity map (Figure 2.4), where you may see the polarized/dichotomized discursive *battlefield* of different team identities (Field Note, 2017c, 2020; Learner Interview, 2018a, 2018b, 2019a, 2019b). This helps to describe the existing positions that can be produced as team identities (for example, Communal Team of Teampreneurs, Team of individuals, Team of Entrepreneurs, Team of Students, Team of makers/ doers). This means that the team produces themselves as,

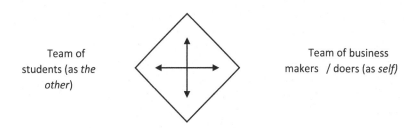

Figure 2.4 Team identity map.

Source: Author's own.

say a *communal team* (which is valuated community ideal as *us/self*), to communicate wanting to be or become one. Still, this (and every) produced meaning is usually unstable, diverse, and changing – team members feel differently about the team identity and the personal significance of the team at any given moment – it is through participative and active dialogue that the team constructs and agrees on their desired meanings: practices, norms, goals, plans, actions, and ideas that also produce identity work. The challenge is that the teams are not born united, but more often stay diverse and increasingly specialize (focus on their own/small group projects), which makes the team identity a choir of dissonant voices.

Team identity builds from shared experiences – through them they receive *identity capital* or at least potential to produce their identity as a team of their making (for example, *communal team*). You may notice that presented identity positions are general, and they don't identify what these identities can *do*. There are no *carpenters*, *nurses,* or *software architects*. Professional identity, excluding *entrepreneurship*, is left open. It eventually leads to the production of entrepreneurs (variation between 20% and 40% of graduates; see Ruuska, 2013), but more than half of the graduates are employed in various business organizations, for example in marketing, sales, and customer service.

How do teams then develop? During the eight years as a team coach, it has been possible to identify a generic pattern (Field Note, 2017c, 2018; Learning Narratives 1–22), that is also saturated in the Learner Interviews (2018a, 2018b, 2019a, 2019b; Learner Interviews 1–14). This model is a theoretical description, based on qualitative data. There are exceptions and applications to present generic patterns that will be discussed more in detail in the doctoral thesis (Ruuska, 2021). The archetypal team development process follows the next five stages (Table 2.1).

What are the requirements for individuals to be a part of the team? This generally becomes a crucial topic of team dialogue, negotiation, and conflict as the teams develop, especially after the *honeymoon*, which I call the *adaptation* phase. After (enthusiastically) learning (many times) about the *new school* values, norms, practices, and teammates, individuals transition to the evaluation phase, where they evaluate the suitability and benefits of the environment to their personal/professional (learning) goals and identity process. This critical phase happens usually simultaneously when the team is struggling with its direction and identity, and usually is missing a purpose or shared goal.[17] This is when some team members leave the team/switch to another study programme. In Tiimiakatemia Jyväskylä rhetoric, this critical phase is called *pseudo team* phase (Katzenbach's & Smith, 1993). When listening to the dialogue and evaluative reflection of team members, the experience of transition from *pseudo team* to *potential team, real team* or

Table 2.1 The archetypal team development process in Tiimiakatemia (Jyväskylä)

Adaptation phase	Open, communal, and enthusiastic, get to know teammates, *learning how it works*
Evaluation and questioning phase	Evaluation of personal gains/team/community identification, *does it work for me/us?*
Team identity construction/ deconstruction phase	Sense of similarity, familiarity, partnership (friendship) and acceptance, shared identity and goals, common practices and norms diverse and/or dissonant phase, as team identity construction is dynamic, incomplete, and contradictory. It is also a field of manipulation, hegemony (leadership/rule) and exercising of power, *learning who I am/who we are*
Construction and specialization phase	Focusing on self-actualization, projects, forming resonating, vital, and supporting groups (overlapping with phase 3). *Learning what I/we will do*
Graduation phase	Graduation from Tiimiakatemia, termination of the cooperative, say goodbye, transformation of identity (alumni-network, moving to *working life)*, embark on a world around trip, *learning who I am (reflective/future orientation). Transition to the future and real life*

Source: Author's own.

high-performance team seems to remain a mystery to the team members, or the shared reflection and identification of the transition is missing or superficial. On the other hand, there are no explicit criteria for any team identity mentioned, but still, these categorical meanings seem to be objectified, included in the team ideology (legitimized) and actively used without much reflection (Document, 2018; Field Note, 2018; Berger & Luckmann, 1966; Aittola, 2012, pp. 62–68).

The discourse on *trust* is a central theme throughout the development process, and when describing an ideal team and team members, the discourse calls for a special kind of trust, that *demands the team members to lay down the shield and believe that no one is going to use their weaknesses or sensitive information against them.* This means that team members should be open about their vulnerability and weaknesses, failures in personal relationships, mistakes, and appeal for help (Lencioni, 2014, p. 204). Lencioni's self-help literature (that is appreciated in Tiimiakatemia) might scratch the surface of the dysfunctions of a team, but it doesn't help beginner teams truly build trust and identity, as trust is a complex concept, takes time to build, and the interpretation of such team development process is easily one-eyed and too-often negative[18] in a very complex social setting (Field Note, 2018; Learner Interview, 2018a, 2018b, 2019a, 2019b).

The criteria for constructing ideal teams seem high, and so are the risks, especially when the formation of a team in Tiimiakatemia includes no common natural reason other than learning (entrepreneurship). What are the odds you wish to absolutely *commit*[19] yourself to a team which is near-randomly formed, and the decision of formation has not been in your power? Also, the concept of trust contains a wide range of meanings that are not self-explanatory and is also related to the concepts of social (and cultural) capital and social networks, which are also useful concepts when describing Tiimiakatemia learning culture (Coleman, 1990; Putnam, 2000; Ilmonen, 2004, pp. 99–142; Bourdieu, 1984).

The previous discourses are central especially in the *Team identity construction/deconstruction* phase, which emphasizes the dialectic and dynamic nature of team identity (as any social) construction and has an effect on the direction of team identity construction – it can construct and deconstruct simultaneously. This phase might overlap with the *construction and specialization* phase, where typically the formulation of smaller, focused groups are formed inside the team, based on different interests and goals. *Graduation* phase ends the team process and serves as a transitional phase for individual identities to *graduate* and move into the future (working life).

Learners Dissonant Identities: Six Learning Personas

In the context of applied ethnography and service design, I suggest six learning personas (Figure 2.5), based on the qualitative data of the research. Learner persona here is thought to be equivalent to *user persona*, which represents the typical/archetypal users of Tiimiakatemia. In the field of product-, interaction-, software, service design and marketing,

1. Paula, Community Active, Teampreneur
6. Elina, Student, Follower-Worker
2. Harri, Creative Dreamer
Dialogue
5. Johannes, Learning Challenges
3. Anna, Practical Maker
4. Jimi, Entrepreneur

Figure 2.5 Six learner personas.

Source: Author's own.

user personas are generally used to communicate values, behaviours, goals, and needs of different types of users (Guðjónsdóttir, 2010; Sissors, 1966; Moore, 1991; Upshaw, 1995; Weinstein, 1998; Mello, 2002; Holtzblatt et al., 2005). Usually, the purpose of creating the personas is practical – to achieve design goals. In this case, the purpose is to offer archetypes for the researchers and designers of communal learning experiences to support understanding different learner needs. In this research, design for all principles (Design for All Europe, 2020) or universal design principles are the motivation for construction of the six personas, not just selecting the *promising* learners. This means ultimately trying to offer the best learning environment for everyone, which, I believe is also an important value in Finnish higher education.

User personas should not be understood as natural persons or deterministic *truths* of their formal status,[20] identity, or the behaviour of a given persona in the cultural context, but data informed representations of social/cultural identity, that can be used to construct scenarios and user stories, that show the potential of a persona's values/needs (what is meaningful to them), goals, strengths, and challenges in the cultural context of Tiimiakatemia. The learners might then behave differently in another learning context or social group. So, the learner personas suggest certain *potential actions, mental models, discourses, or events* in the learners' journey that are happening or can happen. In Service Design context, personas are not constructed to predict user behaviour, but they are used for evaluation, improving, or designing a new service. They can also be used in scenario building, complementing the personas describing how their needs can be met (Hämäläinen & Vilkka, 2010; Guðjónsdóttir, 2010).

The six learner personas are constructed for a special setting of team and communal learning (Tiimiakatemia) and also enable a theoretical construction of the learning community through the (individual) personas. The personas are fictional in the sense that they are representations of the research data, and do not represent any natural persons.[21] Methodologically, this does not differ from typical qualitative data interpretation, which classifies data according to the researcher's interpretation. The difference is only in the type of representation of the data – presenting the data as personas help to understand the types and learner differences in Tiimiakatemia. If you imagine these personas in a team, you can build scenarios or reconstructions of team processes or individuals in a team process and see potential challenges of the learner (Table 2.2).

In Table 2.1, you may see more accurate thematizations of the learner personas. The categories and content have been developed through in-depth themed interviews of the learners[22]and by comparing them to field notes of

Table 2.2 Thematic analysis of the learner personas

Name	Meaningful	Learning goal	Strategy (how to achieve goal)	Strengths	Challenge/risk
Paula, Community Active	Sense of belonging, teamwork	Team formation, team entrepreneurship	Work as a team (in the beginning), focused small group (later)	Social communication and leadership skills	Strategic learning skills, understanding diversity, burnout
Harri, Creative Dreamer	Self-actualization (of dreams)	Becoming yourself, learning, graduation	Focusing on *becoming yourself* – project	Creativity, curiosity, inner motivation, focused	Strategic learning skills, too challenging goals, lack of support
Anna, Practical Maker	Practical work and learning-by-doing	Develop competence (specialization), graduation	Working, learning-by-doing and focusing on projects	Focusing and commitment on personal interests/ practical project work	Academic learning skills, strategic learning skills, communal team learning
Jimi, Entrepreneur	Achieving entrepreneurial and financial goals	Entrepreneurship, serial entrepreneurship	Experimentation in practice	Ability to put ideas into practice and get results	Communal/team learning, exclusion, dropout
Johannes, Learning Challenges	Well-being, being appreciated/ accepted, graduation	Challenges in setting goals, graduation	Be part of projects, study as defined/ instructed	Committed at the beginning of the process	Strategic learning skills, academic/ practical learning, burnout, exclusion, dropout
Elina, Student-Follower-Worker	Sense of belonging, student life, studying successfully	Graduation, grades, university/master studies	Studying successfully, work as instructed	Academic learning skills, self-directive in given context, social	Strategic learning skills, practical learning, setting meaningful goals

Source: Author's own.

72 learners, that I have coached personally for 2.5–3.5 years. The thematic analysis has been holistically evaluated by going through field notes (Field Notes and Training Diaries 2012–2020).

The theme *meaningful* stands for defining briefly, what is and has been meaningful for the learner. In the theme interviews, the learners presented visual narratives, where they identified meaningful events. In addition to this, the quality (or focus) of learners' actions showed meaningfulness also when they didn't label the meaning. *Learning goal* describes the essential goal of the persona, as *Strategy* stands for how to achieve the learning goal. *Strengths* and *Weaknesses* as learners have been analysed especially through field notes, student documents, also integrating analysis from thematic interviews.

Reflections

The research findings presented in this chapter show that Tiimiakatemia learning culture produces itself as a *community* of *similar and diverse beginners*, who construct themselves towards multiple identities, including entrepreneurship. It is a contradictory community, as it creates a platform for communal learning, creativity, and value creation, but teams and the community have a potential to also decrease it. It might not be easily controlled through team coaching without understanding the socially constructed ideologies behind the learning culture, but hopefully this chapter builds awareness to continue the development of such learning cultures, that nurture critical dialogue, openness, and the inclusion of diversity into creativity.

Notes

1. Team Academy, Degree programme in Entrepreneurship at JAMK University of Applied Sciences, Jyväskylä, Finland.
2. Curriculum was changed in 2016, and after that 1st year was dedicated to "basic studies" taught in "traditional" way including basic business courses.
3. I'm using the concept of team identity to describe the process of constructive interplay of individuals and their team, that includes the ways of individuals being and acting (learning) as a part of their team and giving meaning to their shared enterprise.
4. In the domains of contemporary culture research, education, and service design.
5. I will use the neutral term "learner" equivalent to students/teampreneurs.
6. The community size has varied from ≈120 to 70 and back between 2012 and 2020.
7. They are both students and entrepreneurs.
8. Simulating "working life" culture instead of studying.
9. Visiting each other's training sessions.

10. Tiimiakatemia cruise, rocket days.
11. Houston calling, strategy days, kickoff, day of torture (last day of semester) learning circus, Tiimiakatemia birthday.
12. Vision, mission, and values (conveyed especially through leadership program).
13. Brand/marketing manager, alumni manager, recruiting manager, and visiting manager.
14. Communal events of Tiimiakatemia can be seen to carry anthropological forms of play, festival-like events, rituals, and theatrical performances.
15. Leadership/social roles in teams simulate traditional roles in business organisation: Team leader (rental-team leader for first-yearers), financial manager, customer manager, marketing manager and communication manager. Leaders and manager form the board/steering group. Sometimes teams also decide not to select board members in order everyone to take responsibility.
16. On self and the other, see Berger & Luckmann, 1966; Bauman, 1991; and Hall, 1992.
17. It is vital to understand that teams in tiimiakatemia have been created by the team coaches just by using a team role test. There is no other social-, competence- or interest-based process when forming the teams.
18. Concentrating on the dysfunctions, identifying pseudo-teams.
19. *Commitment* is another central concept in team discourse, in "high-communal" team, the requirement of absolute commitment is an ideal or even a norm (despite of what are the team goals).
20. As learners investigated here are all students and entrepreneurs.
21. Still, it is important to mention that the persona gender selections are based on the empirical research data, but are flexible – in other words, personas are not gender-specific.
22. Which of seven I haven't/7 I have a coached for 3.5 years.

References

Research Data

Field Note. (2017a). Everyday -work of a team entrepreneur. 18.1.2017.
Field Note. (2017b). 24-hour -birthgiving, Wire. 16.11.2017.
Field Note. (2017c). On team process. 12.12.2017.
Field Note. (2018). Team development. 18.1.2018.
Field Note. (2019). Tiimiakatemia bubble. 15.3.2019.
Learner Interview. (2018a). 16.3.2018.
Learner Interview. (2018b). 6.4.2018.
Learner Interview. (2019a). 22.2.2019.
Learner Interview. (2019b). 29.1.2019.
Learner Narratives 1–22. (16.12.2016; 4.12.2018; 11.12.2018).

Articles and Books

Aittola, T. (2012). Peter Berger ja Thomas Luckmann: Todellisuuden sosiaalinen rakentuminen, legitimaatio ja sosialisaatio: Teoksessa Kasvatussosiologian suunnannäyttäjiä, Aittola, T. (toim.). (Original – Peter Berger and Thomas Luckmann: The construction of reality, legitimation and socialisation). In T. Aittola (Ed.), *Trendsetters in the sociology of education* (pp. 57–74). Gaudeamus. https://doi.org/10.14361/9783839413272-008

Bauman, Z. (1991). *Modernity and ambivalence*. Polity Press.

Berger, P., & Luckmann, T. (1966). *The social construction of reality: A treatise in the sociology of knowledge*. Penguin.

Bourdieu, P. (1984.) *Distinction: A social critique of the judgement of taste*. Routledge.

Coleman, J. (1990). *Foundations of social theory*. Cambridge University Press.

Cunningham, I. (1999). *The wisdom of strategic learning: The self-managed learning solution (2nd ed)*. Hampshire, UK: Gower Publishing.

Design for All Europe. (2020). Retrieved on January 14, 2021, from https://dfaeurope.eu

Fornäs, J. (1995). *Cultural theory and late modernity 1995*. Sage.

Grogan, J. (2013). *Encountering America: Humanistic psychology, sixties culture, and the shaping of the modern self*. Harper Perennial.

Guðjónsdóttir, R. (2010). *Personas and scenarios in use* (Doctoral Thesis, Kungliga Tekniska Högskolan, Human-Computer Interaction, Stockholm, Sweden). Retrieved on November 17, 2020, from www.researchgate.net/publication/282326654_Personas_and_scenarios_in_use

Hall, S. (1992). The west and the rest: Discourse and power. In S. Hall & B. Gieben (Eds.), *Formations of modernity* (pp. 275–332). Polity Press & Open University.

Hämäläinen, K., & Vilkka, H. (2010). Asiakasymmärryksen ja käyttäjätiedon hankkiminen. Teoksessa Miettinen S. (toim.) (2010) Palvelumuotoilu: Uusia menetelmiä käyttäjätiedon hankintaan ja hyödyntämiseen: Teknologiateollisuus (Original – Collection of customer- and user data). In S. Miettinen (Ed.), *Service design: New methods for collecting and developing user data* (pp. 60–71). Helsinki: Teknologiateollisuus.

Holtzblatt, K., Wendell, J., & Wood, S. (2005). *Rapid contextual design: A how-to guide to key techniques for user-centred design*. Morgan Kaufmann Publishers/Elsevier.

Ilmonen, K. (2004). Sosiaalinen pääoma: uusi ihmekäsite vai käyttökelpoinen hypoteesi? Teoksessa Sosiologisia Nykykeskusteluja, Rahkonen Keijo (toim.). Gaudeamus (in Finnish). *Social capital: New concept of a miracle or useful hypothesis?* Gaudeamus, Helsinki University Press.

Isaacs, W. (1999). *Dialogue and the art of thinking together*. Currency, Random House.

Katzenbach, J., & Smith, D. (1993). *The wisdom of teams: Creating the high-performance organisation*. Harper Business Essentials.

Lencioni, P. (2014). *The five dysfunctions of a team: A leadership fable*. Hoboken, NJ: John Wiley & Sons.

Maslow, A. H. (1943). A theory of human motivation. *Psychological Review, 50*(4), 370–396. Retrieved on April 11, 2019, from http://psychclassics.yorku.ca/Maslow/motivation.htm

Mello, S. (2002). *Customer-centric product definition: The key to great product development*. AMACOM.

Moore, G. A. (1991). *Crossing the chasm: Marketing and selling high-tech products to mainstream customers* (Rev ed., 2002). Harper-Collins Publishers.

Partanen, J. (2012). *The team coach's best tools*. Partus, Jyväskylä.

Putnam, R. D. (2000). *Bowling alone: The collapse and revival of American community*. Simon & Schuster.

Ruuska, J. (2021). Yhteisöllisen yrittäjyyden oppimiskulttuuri: Muotoiluetnografinen tutkimus (kesken): Väitöstutkimus: Nykykulttuurin tutkimus, Jyväskylän yliopisto (in Finnish). *Communal learning culture of team entrepreneurship: Design- ethnographical research of Tiimiakatemia (in progress)* (Doctoral Thesis, Contemporary Culture, University of Jyväskylä, Finland).

Ruuska, J., & Krawczyk, P. (2013, May 23–25). Team academy as a learning living lab. In *Proceedings of University Industry Conference*, Amsterdam, Netherlands.

Senge, P. (1990/2006). *The fifth discipline*. Random House.

Sissors, J. Z. (1966). What is a market? *Journal of Marketing, 30*(3), 17–21. https://doi.org/10.2307/1249085

Upshaw, L. (1995). *Building brand identity: A strategy for success in a hostile marketplace*. John Wiley and Sons.

Van Maanen, J. (2011). *Tales of the field: On writing ethnography, (2nd ed)*. London: The University of Chicago Press.

Weinstein, A. (1998). *Defining your market: Winning strategies for high-tech, industrial, and service firms*. Haworth Press.

3 Lost (and Found) in Translation

Alison Fletcher

Unfolding the Map

I could have devoted this chapter to analysing how the peculiar – very peculiar – language of Team Academy (TA) (or more correctly Tiimi-akatemia) can be explored through multiple lenses of social identity theory, language-in-use, and communities of practice.[1]

Or I could have shown how the development of team learning in tertiary education aligns with a Finnish education model contrasting both philo-sophically and in its outcomes with the UK and USA approach referred to as Global Education Reform Movement (GERM).[2]

But then, you can do that for yourselves. In fact, I've helped you along by sticking some good places to start in a couple of endnotes.

Or I could have used my 4500 words to give you a factual account of what I – we – all of us – did to bring TA into the United Kingdom from Finland. Starting with *in November 2010 I was introduced to the concept by a fellow consultant, went to Finland, got excited, trained as a team coach, set up Akatemia CIC, got more people excited, these excited people opened university departments* and ending with? There is no end, so that would be a bit tricky.

And be honest, when you did history at school it wasn't really the dates, reigns and rulers, battles, and beheadings that caught your imagination, was it? (Well, maybe the beheadings. . .). It was the times when you glimpsed our ancestors as three-dimensional humans with passions, vulnerabilities, and idiosyncrasies suspiciously like our own.

Shall we go there? Into one or two of the corners of the past 10 years where you get glimpses of Alison and what she's up to? Our lovely editors assure me there's a research methodology called *autoethnography* and if I succeed in helping you understand the TA process by showing it at work on me, then we can sneak this chapter into the book under that guise.

DOI: 10.4324/9781003163091-4

Plotting the Route

You'll want to know something about me, I would imagine, to make sense of what we share in these pages. A potted biography? A CV? That'll eat up the word count. I tell you what, I'll put a link to my personal website in a footnote for the nuts and bolts.[3]

Now come with me as we head up the Great North Road and over the River Tyne to the city of Newcastle, where I was born in 1957.

Words are my thing. Words and stories. As a small child, I spent most weekends with my grandparents because my mum was struggling to cope with my new baby brother (we didn't talk about post-natal depression in the early 1960s). Grandpa and I would browse through his eclectic library of Victorian and Edwardian literature and makeup stories inspired by our reading. I went home having written a poem for each member of my family and proudly read out these immortal lines to my dad:

He wakes me in the morning light
An angel without wings
But when he's in the bath at night
Oh heavens! How he sings.

Tennyson it wasn't but after his death in 2016 I found that little piece of paper in a five-year-old's writing folded up in my dad's wallet.

Words are my thing. They are my sword and buckler, my armour against the world. Bullied at school, I used words to mock my persecutors and found in humour a way of cutting the bullies down to size. Along with my love of stories came an identification with under-dogs and outsiders, coupled with an immense curiosity about all the things I didn't know. I represented Newcastle in a school debating competition in which I argued – successfully – for the motion that children should be taught skills for life and not just academic subjects.

Which was ironic, as I was the most scatter-brained, impractical teenager you could hope to meet, living in my imagination and nearly getting sacked from my holiday job in a laundry when confused customers got back a motley collection of sheets and towels they'd never seen before.

Something had to be done, and I characteristically chose the nuclear option. I turned my back on a place to read English at university and headed to Newcastle Polytechnic to do a secretarial course. I was going to become efficient and employable, come what may.

That decision at the age of 18 was one of the turning points of my life, although I didn't know it at the time. I hadn't given up on higher education – I would go on to get a degree from Oxford, three postgraduate certificates, and an MSc – but I always retained the sense of detachment that came from being a mature student, an outsider. Unlike my undergraduate peers, I'd worked for four years, I could get well-paid work as a secretary during the holidays, and I had the discipline of going out to work, so I didn't have to pull all-nighters to get my essays done on time. And despite the intellectual stimulation of studying the great works of English literature, I wanted more. I knew there was a big world beyond the dreaming spires, and that to survive out there I would need to know things I couldn't learn from my lectures and tutorials.

In the years after university words would again be my chief source of joy and inspiration as a newspaper journalist, I moved from *doing* to *organizing*, exercising my facility with words to craft stories around our corporate endeavours, build strategies and create shared visions. Ten years as a senior manager in the BBC taught me how to use language for challenge, compromise, collaboration, and conflict resolution.

Why am I bothering to tell you all this and what has it got to do with TA? We're getting there, I promise you.

When I say words are my thing, there are a few non-negotiables we can take as read. 1. No Americanisms. Ever. Colour, not color; meet, not meet with; may I have? not can I get? 2. Grammar and spelling are sacrosanct. It's not acceptable to put apostrophe's in the wrong place. 3. English is the most beautiful and flexible language in the world and finding appropriate, elegant, and eloquent ways of saying things is a sacred duty.

So, what happened when the non-negotiables and TA's version of the English language came up against each other?

Learning from real life, using coaching as a tool for learning, developing graduates ready for the world of work – what I heard about TA struck a chord that made me want to know more. And so it was that on 20 January 2011 – almost exactly 10 years ago as I write these words – Robert Goodsell[4] and I embarked on our Learning Expedition to Tiimiakatemia in Jyväskylä, Central Finland, in what would prove to be another life-changing experience (Figure 3.1).

As a trainee teacher, I'd experienced learning as something I did **to** other people. As a coach, it was something I did **for** other people. As a student, it was something I did **for myself**. What I wasn't prepared for, and reacted strongly against, was the realization that in this world learning was something I would have to do **with** other people, that the control would pass out of my hands. I was outed by a self-possessed young Finn who gave me feedback (Me? Feedback?!!) on how she experienced my presence in a group discussion. *I notice you keep going into your head and finding things to be critical about.* Of course, I was in my head; it was the only place I felt remotely safe in this scariest of experiences.

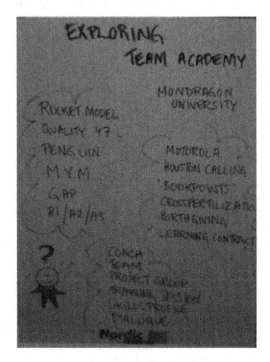

Figure 3.1 Flipchart image of Tiimiakatemia terminology.
Source: Author's own.

But the ideas underpinning this way of learning were not unfamiliar. Working as an executive coach I'd already begun to understand something of the self-authoring power of language. Your story is not just how you communicate with me, it's how you understand yourself. Could **my** story incorporate post-motorolas, birthgivings, forest-and-back, Houston Calling, and a host of other linguistic manglings? Could I learn to become a team entrepreneur?[5]

To answer that question, you're coming with me to Irun, Debrecen, Jyväskylä, and finally back to Newcastle, where the story started. In these places, I wrote a new story. In 2011, I signed up for Team Mastery, the 18-month process designed by Johannes Partanen, founder of Tiimi-akatemia, to train practitioners in his methodology. These extracts from my reflective journal and essays encapsulate what I discovered about myself, team learning, and the power of a shared language to create a community connected by values and goals.

The Journey Begins

May 2011 – Mondragon University in Spain's Basque Country

Watching a training session, I mentally label the participants – shapers, doers, divergers, builders, and sleepers.

The shapers had ideas and added energy; they wanted to move through the process at a brisk pace. The doers got interested when it came to concrete proposals that they could imagine putting into action. Then they came up with ideas for how the practical problems could be addressed.

The divergers were the ones I found most irritating, while accepting that occasionally they added something valuable. They wouldn't stick to the point but kept bringing in other elements, mostly impracticable. The builders were the most helpful. They listened carefully to what was being said and built on the ideas of other people to move the thinking forwards.

The sleepers did just that; sat almost comatose on the fringes, occasionally consulting their phones but otherwise seemingly oblivious to what was going on.

There were complaints that things were going missing from the office; people weren't respecting possessions, and they couldn't agree about how to buy stationery. This reminded me of the banality of so many of the problems that characterize the modern workplace; co-workers are more likely to fall out because someone has used someone else's mug or parking space than because a work deadline has been missed.

The session took a surprising direction when one of the *sleepers* came to life and asked a penetrating question: What are our priorities? What matters most and what doesn't matter as much?

This challenged the assumptions I'd been making; that he wasn't interested or engaged in the process. I saw what I hadn't seen; the level of stress beneath the surface, the frustration with battling to get things done in a big group, the conflicting pressures of academic work and TA processes. A group is a group, but it is also made up of individuals, all with their own hopes and fears.

I'd like to think that I had that in mind when we went back into our teams in the afternoon to work on our presentations for the evening's birth-giving. But in the first hour, I reverted to my preferred team type and kept pushing to converge, resolve, distill, and agree actions. I felt increasingly frustrated with the divergent voices in the team and could feel myself disengaging.

I saw elements of the same stress and frustration that I'd observed in the training session. The team was not yet a team, just a disparate group of individuals with their own ideas, preconceptions, and wants. A couple of people felt very uncomfortable with the task itself and couldn't step outside their discomfort and allow the process to unfold. The energy levels were dropping as we sat in the room feeling frustrated with each other.

Reflecting on the moment I reminded myself that I was there to learn, to do things differently, to challenge my preferred style, and push myself to my edge. If the task didn't get done, that in itself would be a learning experience.

Getting outside and being playful about going on a boat trip to a different country (across the river which formed the border between Spain and France), allowed the group to step into a more creative energy. As I became less driven about getting things done, a colleague picked up the pace and managed the time. When everyone had a task, we worked as a purposeful unit. I saw that when people have roles they feel appreciated and secure. It's easier to give people roles when you move to action; more challenging when you're in the thinking phase.

The birth-giving, about which I'd been cynical and dismissive, was a bonding experience, and watching other people's presentations revealed the diversity and depth of talent in the whole group. I saw how important it is for the coach to trust in the members of the team, their personalities and creativity. As a team-member, this will be my biggest challenge. Trusting the process, trusting myself, that I will know when to speak and when to keep silent, when to hold back, and when to keep pushing in the knowledge that my contribution is something that will enhance the quality of the group's output.

My first experience of dialogue was tough. I almost exploded internally with irritation at a late-comer and looked about me with disgruntled unease at the strange faces. At the same time, I didn't want to show how I was feeling and as a consequence I could feel my face setting into a smile that felt false.

All very familiar – I find group learning stressful and have on occasions sabotaged my own learning because of it. I noticed how my engagement flicked on and off, how quickly bored I became and how hard it was to really listen. How many other people in the group were feeling the same? I thought of the phrase "surfing the discomfort" and remembered a client who had an image of moving through life like jumping out of a plane; you can't defy gravity and do anything but fall, but what you can choose is what shape you're going to make on the way down.

What shape do I want to make?

Team Leadership and Tortoises

Returning to Jyväskylä as a team mastery participant gave me the chance to work with a first-year team company, which was struggling with how to choose a leader and what that leader should be doing. Social neuroscience suggests in our social interactions just as in our primitive battle for survival we are predominantly driven by the principal of minimizing Threat and maximizing Reward.[6] At the formation of the team company, there is a vacuum in the space called leadership. People don't know much about leading themselves; they know less about leading others and nothing at all about leading a business. As a result, the Threat response is activated when they are brought together to achieve a joint purpose.

When we experience a Threat, we have four basic responses – Fight, Flight, Freeze, and Flock.[7] I'm thinking about the last of these – Flock – and the behaviour of penguins (first years) in new TA intakes. I also saw plenty of Freezing, as people made themselves as still and insignificant as possible to avoid being singled out for attention. I wonder if we all have preferred responses or use the four strategies interchangeably depending on the circumstances?

A theme around responsibility runs through reflections from Jyväskylä; responsibility for self, for the group, for the learning, and for the community. It's also about being passionate, speaking from the heart, and being clear about what we care about. In the Threat/Reward dichotomy, I can see that this means making a choice not to be driven by Threat response, but engaging with the Reward of our over-arching goal, whatever that may be; our vision for how TA can shape our futures and those of the young people we are going to work with.

In this module, the shape I made was mostly a tortoise. My head and legs came out in the sunshine of agreeable social interactions but withdrew smartly when the group became uncomfortable, or I was tired, or bored, or irritated. I can see this was threat-based behaviour, driven to minimize ambiguity, discomfort around not knowing what to do, and disagreements about our direction. But occasionally, I left the shell and when I did, I found I could move more freely without it.

How to make the experience of Team Mastery about reward rather than the avoidance of threat? What shape would that need to be? Perhaps, caterpillar turning into a moth. At the moment, I'm still a caterpillar and my skin feels too tight, I want to fly but can't and I'm called upon to do things I don't know how to do. Can I become a moth more quickly? Probably not, but I can practice moth-type thinking. What would the Alison-moth do in this situation? What is already available to me? What is the next step in the moth journey and what will help me take it?

No more tortoises.

Being Brave in Hungary

This was my first module without Robert, and I hadn't realized how much I would miss his calm, reassuring presence. Robert knows the language of international travel like he knows how to put on his socks. I felt a long way from home as I made my way to the Budapest station. But on the train, there was a dining car, and in the dining car was a waitress, and the waitress was one of those characters who burst out of daily life and remind you that you are alive. By this stage, I knew in my head that I was starting to have fun, but I didn't fully experience the fun until she arrived. Her improbably bright-dyed hair, her constant stream of Hungarian modulated only by the fact that she'd lost her voice and was reduced to a croak and the smile that played on her lips as she watched the people of four nations sample her palinka all said: *Stop. Savour this moment. Be here with me now*. And in choosing to fully be there I felt real camaraderie with the group, a shared purpose, a sense of responsibility both for and to them, wanting to give as well as receive.

I was intrigued by a conversation with another coach, who felt she and her colleague had in some way built teams that reflected their own person-alities. If our personalities not only affect how we coach but the style of team we develop, then we need a level of awareness to see the impact we are having. If I want my team to make authentic, brave, and resourceful choices then that suggests that it is not only what I do but how I am that will influ-ence this. This reminded me of a comment by one of the team entrepreneurs in Finland: "You have to be brave enough to make demands of your team members and to hold them to account."

Looking back on the group process, where I took a big step forward in understanding my place and purpose, we experienced the need for authen-ticity and bravery in managing a conflict with a fellow group member. Tak-ing care of the process so that the team can develop is the responsibility of everyone, not just the coach or even the leader.

What did I learn? Listening – offering the space with curiosity and atten-tion; Performing even when I am at my lowest; Being aware of cultural differences but not straight-jacketed by them; Appreciating my own unique gifts and being generous with how I share them.

How then do we coach the capacity to make good choices? We lead by example; we are role models in the way we behave and respond to chal-lenges. We encourage others by showing we are willing to make difficult choices and not be afraid of the consequences. To make good choices requires good quality thinking and as coaches we can encourage others to think more creatively, deeply, and rigorously by paying attention and keep-ing the process in view.

And what shape did I make in Hungary? I know it was something with four legs, but no shell. A large woolly dog is in my mind. I came across this breed of Hungarian flock guard dog, the Kuvasz, and loved the way it was described; brave enough to drive off a wolf or a bear which threatened its flock, yet so gentle that it would look after the ewes in labour and make sure the new-born lambs could find their mothers. Not a bad role model!

How to Build a Bridge

Our module in Newcastle upon Tyne was a powerful reconnection with my roots and values. Here, I was able to bring together what I'd learned about myself, my understanding of TA, and the work Robert and I had done over the past year to build a coalition of courageous people who were now on the way to launching degree programmes in three universities in England. In my reflections, I used the construction of the Tyne Bridge as a metaphor for building the TA community in the United Kingdom.

Figure 3.2 is a still image from a video that shows the completion of the Tyne Bridge in 1928 by a local contractor who later went on to build the Sidney Harbour Bridge. Its design mirrors its bigger, younger, and more famous brother, and at that time, it was the biggest single span bridge in the world.[8]

Look at the way the bridge starts at either end, slowly advancing forwards and upwards until the two halves meet in the middle as a perfect arch. See the men balance precariously as the suspension wires are tightened.

Figure 3.2 Completion of the Tyne Bridge, 1928
Source: Courtesy of the BFI National Archive.

They know what they're doing, but the work is dangerous, and one man died during the construction.

And you can design all you like, you can work as hard as you are physically able, but you never quite know, never quite know, that the two halves are going to meet.

The bridge is my metaphor for our work over the past 10 years. And this is my formula for how to build a bridge.

Know Why You Want a Bridge in the First Place

The Tyne Bridge heralded the new era of the motor car and carried the Great North Road from London to Edinburgh. It meant communication, connection, speed, and ambition. In physical form, it made manifest the pride, ingenuity, and technical brilliance of Northern engineers. The reason for your bridge should be bigger than the bridge – so for a big bridge, you need big reasons.

Pick Your Spot

This was the place chosen by the Romans for their original Pons Aelius which saw the birth of Newcastle as a settlement. You have to go a long way to better the Romans in decision-making. Learn from others, copy them if necessary.

Envision Your Final Structure

See it, feel it, hear how it sounds with the wind blowing through it, and taste the metal in the air. Let it be the stuff of your dreams. Picture it when you go to sleep and meet it when you wake.

Detail, Detail, Detail

Some of us love it. Others hate it. Know which type of person you are and surround yourself with people of the opposite persuasion. They will drive you mad. Without them, you will fail.

Recruit Your Bridge-Builders

Strong women (the Tyne Bridge team included Dorothy Buchanan, the first female member of the Institute of Civil Engineers) and men, resilient, practical, hard-working, serious about the task but with humour to deflect the everyday annoyances of building your bridge. They must have the balance to work at heights, be good at working together even when they can't hear or see each other and above all believe that the perfect arch is achievable.

Leave Them to Get On With It

Don't be for ever tinkering. Trust that they know what they are doing but give them encouragement and support when the rain is lashing down, the wind is howling, and the steel won't cooperate. A beer at the end of the day doesn't go amiss.

Believe in Your Design

You know what you are doing. The design is good. The people are the right people. It is the right bridge in the right place. The arch will meet.

Now you have built your bridge. Take time to savour it. This moment is unique, never to be repeated. Something has been born.

The End and the Beginning

The baby that was born 10 years ago has itself given birth to 11 under-graduate and post-graduate degree programmes (eight still running) with two more in the pipeline and others in development; 90 prospective team coaches have followed in my footsteps to train in the team mastery process in our own UK Team Mastery. Supported by Akatemia Community Interest Company (strapline Team Learning), the methodology has been used in community projects, organizations, and school classrooms. The global pandemic that caused so much disruption to education also opened up new opportunities for virtual collaboration on a national and international scale. To date, over 200 young people from six countries and three continents have participated in the Akatemia Global Business Challenge, juggling technology, time zones, and cultural differences to evidence the power of working and learning in teams.

Thank you for your company on this journey. And if you are one of the many, many people who have been bridge-building with us over the past 10 years, thank you for your patience, energy, commitment, and companionship.

Notes

1. Eckert, P. (2006). Communities of practice. In K. Brown (Ed.), *Encyclopaedia of language and linguistics* (2nd ed., pp. 683–685). Elsevier Science and Technology Books, Oxford.

Turner, J. C., & Reynolds, K. J. (2010). The story of social identity. In T. Postmes & N. Branscombe (Eds.), *Rediscovering social identity: Core sources* (pp. 142–146). Psychology Press.

Eastman, C. M. (1985). Establishing social identity through language use. *Journal of Language and Social Psychology*, *4*(1), 1–20.

2. Sahlberg, P. (2005). *Finnish lessons 2.0* (2nd ed.). Teachers' College Press, Columbia.
3. www.thecoachwithin.co.uk/about/
4. Robert Goodsell, my co-director and founder of Akatemia CIC, who was also a participant on Team Mastery. https://akatemia.org.uk/who-we-are/
5. More on the language of Team Academy can be found in The Team Coach's Best Tools by Johannes Partanen (2016), ISBN 978–952–67208–9–0
6. Rock, D. (2020). *Your brain at work*. HarperCollins.
7. Rock, D. (2020). *Your brain at work*. HarperCollins.
8. www.youtube.com/watch?v=MfcyDejA6Ek&feature=related

References

Eastman, C. M. (1985). Establishing social identity through language use. *Journal of Language and Social Psychology*, *4*(1), 1–20.

Eckert, P. (2006). Communities of practice. In K. Brown (Ed.), *Encyclopaedia of language and linguistics* (2nd ed., pp. 683–685). Elsevier Science and Technology Books, Oxford.

Partanen, J. (2016). *The team coach's best tools*. Partus, Jyväskylä.

Sahlberg, P. (2005). *Finnish lessons 2.0* (2nd ed.). Teachers' College Press, Columbia.

Turner, J. C., & Reynolds, K. J. (2010). The story of social identity. In T. Postmes & N. Branscombe (Eds.), *Rediscovering social identity: Core sources* (pp. 142–146). Psychology Press.

4 Innovation Within the Lines

Implementation of a Bachelor of Science in Entrepreneurship and Strategic Networking

Sophia Koustas and Susan Losapio

Introduction

This chapter overviews the learning journey of the authors, who set out to implement an innovative entrepreneurship program that meets institutional and national educational standards, program accreditation, and branding guidelines. The Higher Education industry is constantly changing and evolving (LeBlanc, 2018). Therefore, University College and School of Business leadership at Southern New Hampshire University (SNHU) identified the need to be innovative in order to stay competitive. A new Dean for the School of Business was hired in July 2017 to lead the school through a re-visioning process. In June 2018, administrators and key faculty members embarked on a *learning journey* to research, observe, and benchmark different pedagogical practices of the Team Academy (TA) framework around the world (Fowle & Jussila, 2016; Ruuska & Krawczyk, 2013; Tosey et al., 2015). Participating in the AKATEMIA[1] Team Mastery Coaching program provided additional opportunities for professional development at an international level (Working to learn, 2020). The culmination of this knowledge, along with the institutional support, inspired the development of the innovative Bachelor of Science in Entrepreneurship (BS.ENT) using the team-based experiential academic model (t.e.a.m.). Utilizing strategic networking was grounded in inclusivity, communication, and collaboration led to university-wide support and the ability to overcome potential obstacles and resistance.

To organize the journey of developing a BS.ENT degree at SNHU, multiple creative and innovative tools were used. For this chapter, the Innovation Dice™ (Inno-Zone, 2021) is utilized for explaining the process of innovating a new degree program that although needs to follow specific requirements (between the lines) was designed using an "outside of the box" approach. The Innovation Dice™ utilizes the six phases – identify, insight, inspire, ideate, impact, and innovation – which incorporate commonalities

DOI: 10.4324/9781003163091-5

of various models in the literature review and aligns with the natural process that emerged while designing the new degree program at SNHU.

Literature Review

For innovation to flourish, transformational leadership complemented by group innovative behaviour fosters the emergence of an innovative eco-system (Feng et al., 2016). Following a specific process for innovation is a way to gain buy-in and excitement from key stakeholders (Hansen et al., 2019). Innovation has taken many different forms over the years with distinct phases and/or stages. The most frequently referenced phases are identifying the problem, ideating, and implementing the idea (Amabile, 1996; Mumford et al., 1991; Treffinger & Isaksen, 1992).

A common starting point is to identify an unmet need or problem within an industry or marketplace (Baggen et al., 2015; Edelbroek et al., 2019; Medeiros et al., 2018; Price & Wrigley, 2016). The term "identify" may also refer to entrepreneurial opportunities potentially leading to new products, services, or innovation using a customer-centric approach (Baggen et al., 2015). The outcome of this phase is to clearly state the need or problem being addressed by concisely writing a statement to transition to the next phase, which is insight.

The insight phase is characterized by information gathering, preparation, and internal and external assessment. The focus is to clearly understand the unmet need or problem by determining what is already known and what can be easily learned (Huang et al., 2020; Medeiros et al., 2018). Insight methods are mentioned in the literature in relation to the customer experience and better understanding of their needs (Price & Wrigley, 2016). An additional perspective involves gauging the culture of the company driving the innovation. According to Senge (1990), an advocate of the TA framework, a learning organization has a culture that embraces innovation due to the consistent assessment of policies and practices. Gaining knowledge and collecting multiple insights can be accomplished through different methods including persona design, storytelling, customer narratives, scenarios, co-design, touchpoint timeline, and shadowing (Price & Wrigley, 2016). This base of knowledge is used to determine sources of inspiration, which is the third phase.

The inspiration phase involves the consideration of new perspectives, best practices, different industries, and unrelated products and/or events to assist in moving from what is known to what can be created (Chan et al., 2015; Crilly & Cardoso, 2017; Seonghoon et al., 2018; Sio et al., 2015). Benchmarking and thinking outside of the box truly untethered the innovation process from currently used practices. To be clear, this is not the brainstorming or ideation phase. This is part of the data gathering process; brainstorming occurs next in phase four, ideation.

The work done in all the previous phases helps make ideation a creative and exhilarating experience. Furthermore, beyond generating multiple ideas, the focus is on grouping, identifying patterns, and seeking commonalities. It is also possible that newer problems, entrepreneurial opportunities, or unmet needs may be discovered and therefore bring the process of innovation back to the identification phase (Medeiros et al., 2018; Huang et al., 2020). Once the idea is fully formed, the next phase is to assess its impact on the internal and external environments of the institution.

Impact includes the actual planning for the realization of the idea, from time planning, to resource planning, including developing prototypes and testing (Bolland, 2020). Part of the process is to move an idea into an opportunity by assessing its impact on an organization. For example, knowledge of consumer impact factors, acceptance within the marketplace, anticipated value, and potential risk factors (Albertsen et al., 2020) can all be considered. Although impact assessment is highlighted as phase five, it is also threaded throughout the innovation process by reviewing stakeholder engagement, employee motivation, evaluation of the ideation, and scalability of the innovation (Aragon et al., 2017). Innovation can become embedded and capitalized upon "by stimulating knowledge sharing within and across organizations" (Edelbroek, 2019, p. 6). An idea only becomes an innovation if it is applied to the real world. Otherwise, it is, and remains, "only" a good idea (Bolland, 2020). Hence, careful consideration of the impact and related factors will lead to the final phase which is innovation.

The final phase of innovation draws upon all the information obtained above to determine the best way to launch the new product or service. According to Glor (2014), an organization should focus not only on the creative process but also on the long-term financial health and viability of the innovation. This will ensure adding value to the organization and obtaining greater stakeholder buy-in of the implementation plan for the innovation.

Overall, the first three phases are about diverging, from identifying the challenge via gaining insights and inspiration (Bolland, 2020; Kelley & Kelley, 2013). The last three phases involve converging from developing ideas to selecting these and deciding what it will take to realize them, implement, prototype, test, and finally create the innovation. In fact, the borders are not razor blade sharp. This innovation now forms an answer to the design challenge (Bolland, 2020). The innovation journey is from question (identify) to answer (innovation), or simply, "innovation is a journey from knowing, via not knowing, to new knowing" (Bolland, 2020).

Implementation of the BS.ENT and Strategic Networking at SNHU

The implementation of the BS.ENT was planned for fall 2020. Leadership decided that due to the current COVID-19 uncertainty, it would be best to postpone the launch until fall 2021. This shift of events allowed the faculty champions to embrace an opportunity and focus on designing an entrepreneurship program that is interoperable across the institution's units and provides learners with options of engaging in practical experiences.

The Innovation Dice™ at SNHU

The Innovation Dice™, inspired by André Bolland (Inno-Zone, 2021), became the blueprint to explain the innovation process used to develop the BS.ENT degree. In this section, each phase is presented first by identifying the question(s) to be answered, followed by a brief explanation of what is required, an example of its application in the case of SNHU, and a reflection on the main takeaways.

Identify – What Is the Challenge?

The innovation process starts with identifying a trend, need, or desire in a given market. The goal of the innovator(s) is to formulate a "sharp question" that considers leadership buy-in, adequate time, specific unambiguous language, and understands the challenge to be solved. A *sharp* question needs to be clearly expressed and articulated. A sharp question leads to a sharp answer.

Observed higher education institutions (HEIs) trend to include decreased student enrolments, increased competition between institutions, reallocation of government funding, student-centric curriculum, acceptance of competency-based education (CBE), inequities amongst stakeholders, and increased personal and institutional debt (Jacob & Gokbel, 2018). Additionally, other institutional trends may include changing faculty roles, overarching accountability, redistribution of budget, corporatization of the industry, shift in student needs, and opportunities for interactive experiences (Bloom & McClellan, 2016). All these trends clearly lead learners to seek and HEIs to develop programs and educational opportunities that are affordable, learner-centric with a focus on learning-by-doing, which were all evident and common across the observed TAs around the world.

By considering all the above and vetting many renditions, the sharp question identified was: What is an appropriate and effective framework for SNHU to implement in order to provide our learners with opportunities to take control of their own learning and become resilient contributors in their communities?

Insight – What Do We Know?

In this phase, there are some key questions to consider which align with conducting an analysis to review the product/service, industry/target, organizational and financial feasibility (Barringer, 2015) of a new product or service. Consequently, the analysis identifies the three factors of desirability, feasibility, and viability to determine where innovation sparks and *design thinking lives* (Kelley & Kelley, 2013). According to Bolland (2020), a fourth factor, scalability, is also important to consider the opportunities an innovation needs to succeed. The main driver may include understanding the speed at which a product/service can be mass-produced and/or provided based on demand.

WHAT DO WE ALREADY KNOW?

Various factors (social, cultural, technological, political, and economic) have contributed to the "demand" of entrepreneurship (Hart, 2003; Mwasalwiba, 2010). The current student population, millennials, are considered digital natives skilled in technology, social media, and prefer to be their own boss (Abrams, 2017). Entrepreneurship education emerged as a field of study as there was more interest and support from stakeholders, policymakers, academics, and most importantly learners (Mwasalwiba, 2010). Learners do not obtain knowledge in the same way and their preferred learning modalities vary between lecture-based, experiential, and blended learning. HEIs have created entrepreneurship programs that include study and experience of some or several activities (Sirelkhatim & Gangi, 2015). Upon observation, experiential education is core within the TA framework, a trend in academia (Anders, 2019), and a popular option at SNHU. Additionally, SNHU's leadership continues to encourage groups across the university to develop and test opportunities to provide the best and most personalized learner experience. This is accomplished by delivering high-demand credentials leading to meaningful work and purposeful lives and seeking opportunities to future-proof the institution.

WHAT IS OUR COLLECTIVE WISDOM?

For innovation to occur at SNHU, it is essential to have a leader who is passionate, shares the vision, takes calculated risks, assists in removing obstacles, and finds solutions. The Dean for the School of Business embodied all these characteristics and was supportive throughout. Additionally, a guiding coalition was built by inviting key stakeholders in influential positions (for example, School Deans, the Director of the Centre for Teaching and Learning, etc.) to ensure support and alignment of using t.e.a.m. as the preferred pedagogy. By reflecting on the implementation of various innovations at the institution, it became clear that creating stakeholder buy-in and engaging in effective communication was essential. The selected approach involved outreach across the institutional units (departments, schools, services, etc.) to determine the impact of all those involved. Having proactive conversations across the university, facilitated the reduction of potential barriers, opened the communication channels, and fostered a cross-collaborative environment (for example, restrictions of the current learning management system). Communicating and collaborating with the staff who operate this platform ensured a suitable solution.

WHAT CAN WE EASILY FIND OUT?

Observing and benchmarking other SNHU innovations and best TA practices around the world provided the opportunity to gain a greater understanding of related risks, obstacles, opportunities, potential collaborations, and access to resources.

By considering all the above, the two main insights identified were

- utilizing political and human capital is essential for buy-in and
- delivering an inclusive and effective communication strategy decreases resistance.

Inspiration – What Best Practices Exist?

This part of the innovation process focused on seeking sources of inspiration. The benchmarking provided exposure to proven practices, alternative perspectives, and shared norms of innovative entrepreneurship-focused pedagogical models (see Table 4.1).

By considering all the above, the three main sources of inspiration were

- learning through observations;
- engaging in dialogue with team coaches; and
- identifying learner key attributes.

Ideate – What to Do?

Working with a multifaceted and inquisitive group of individuals from different disciplines and departments across an institution will lead to the development of a multitude of ideas. Organizing a series of ideation sessions with stakeholders starts with sharing options and exploring possibilities and concepts for consideration.

Table 4.1 Benchmarking highlights

Locations observed	• Mondragon Team Academy, Spain (June 2018) • Team Academy Amsterdam, Netherlands (June 2018, March 2019) • Tiimiakatemia (Jyväskylä) and Proakatemia (Tampere), Finland (March 2019, September 2019) • Aston University (Birmingham), University West of England (Bristol), UK (January 2019, June 2019, January 2020) • HES-SO (Sierre), Switzerland (November 2019)
Subject Matter Expert (SME) conversation	• Workshop with SNHU faculty and staff members facilitated by TA expert • Communication with other team coaches • Team Mastery Coaching (AKATEMIA), Team4Learning Conference
Observed Culture	• Underlying Assumptions: learner-centric design, ability to learn by doing, interest in entrepreneurship, increase of confidence, trusting the process • Values: accountability, teamwork, trust, diversity, respect • Tangible Artifacts: stories and visuals of success and failing forward, space layout and design, ability to break bread, community spaces, modern design, smart furniture choices, success exhibit areas, access to resources, effective team dynamics, just-in-time learning environment • Intangible Artifacts: failing forward, meaningful dialogue, energetic vibe, and collaborative spirit
Status and structure	• University (co-op, for profit, public, non-profit) • Private institution

Source: Authors' own.

At SNHU, this involved organizing several sessions with faculty and staff with a designated facilitator. A TA coach and expert, André Bolland from TA Amsterdam, facilitated the first session. The following sessions were run in a business challenge format to determine a vision of how an innovative entrepreneurship-focused pedagogy could be incorporated at the School of Business at SNHU. The next two gatherings explored moving the initial ideas into more detail by focusing on curriculum design and key components for each academic year. The report-outs resulted in the observation of several patterns and commonalities leading to a convergence of themes. The themes helped identify the areas of impact to be explored in the next section.

By considering all the above, the four main themes were

• supporting and developing life-long learners;
• pursuing opportunities for community partnerships within SNHU, regionally, nationwide, and abroad;

- encouraging faculty and staff on-campus to explore various learning modalities; and
- creating an innovative, creative, and inclusive learning environment.

Impact – Who and What Is Impacted?

The ideate phase provides awareness of which stakeholders may be missing and *what's next*. Working the themes into something tangible and making the innovation become a reality are key outcomes of the impact phase to confirm the desirability, feasibility, viability, and scalability of the innovation. This involves a review as to how the innovation will impact the institution and the greater community. Possible impact factors include internal and external stakeholders, systems, policies, and procedures, and, ultimately, alignment with the mission of the institution.

At SNHU, the educational process is learner centric. There are numerous systems and people that exist to support the learner's needs (see Figure 4.1). Additionally, consideration of faculty roles is essential to determine course load, contract requirements and restrictions, and alignment with governing bodies (i.e., faculty senate and the collective bargaining association). However, without full commitment from leadership – at all levels – implementation of the innovation could have been met with greater resistance. In fact, resistance was met on three distinct occasions; while requesting to adapt existing curriculum requirements, branding requirements of the innovation, and interoperable program requests (online, on-campus, and hybrid). The reason for the resistance in each case was rooted in traditional practices and corporate guidelines. However, in both cases, a respectful resolution was achieved due to strong upper leadership commitment. Developing partnerships was an integral part of the innovation. Community outreach with potential mentors, investors, and partners brought about several opportunities and challenges. The opportunities included observation of ecosystems, learning about other models, inquiry of support roles, and engagement within an international community. The greatest challenge was the lack of clarity – which may have been in part a cultural nuance – about the legal and monetary requirements and obligations required to implement a similar program at SNHU. Upon further exploration and consultation with SNHU's Legal Counsel, it was decided to move ahead independently and create t.e.a.m. to provide an alternative learning modality for the BS.ENT and other disciplines (i.e., engineering, sport management, gaming, education, and construction management).

By considering all the above, the five ways to create impact were by

- keeping learner needs in the forefront;
- reviewing existing systems to assess resource needs;

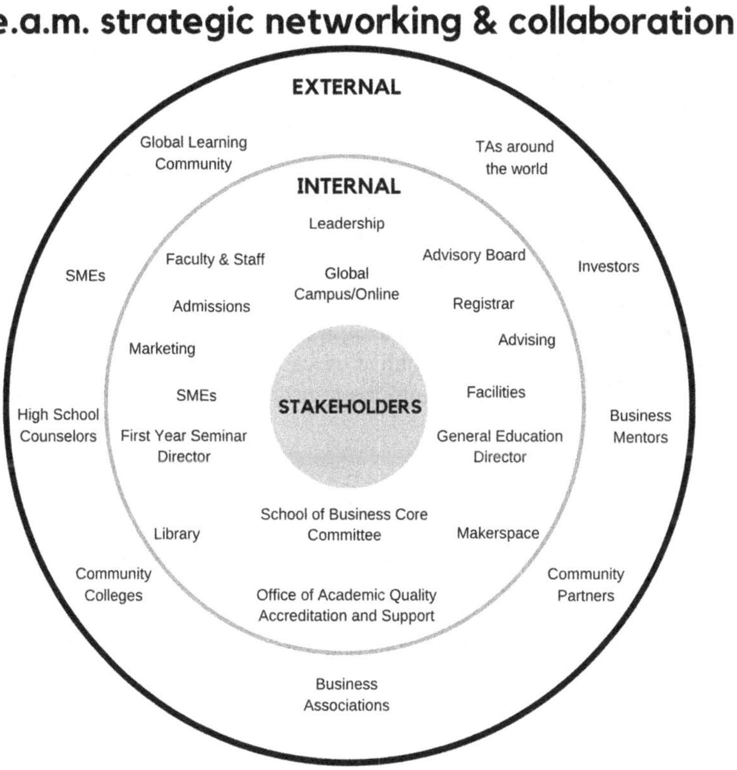

t.e.a.m. strategic networking & collaboration

EXTERNAL

Global Learning Community

TAs around the world

INTERNAL

Leadership

Faculty & Staff

Advisory Board

Investors

SMEs

Global Campus/Online

Admissions

Registrar

Advising

Marketing

SMEs

STAKEHOLDERS

Facilities

High School Counselors

First Year Seminar Director

General Education Director

Business Mentors

School of Business Core Committee

Library

Makerspace

Community Colleges

Office of Academic Quality Accreditation and Support

Community Partners

Business Associations

Figure 4.1 Strategic networking and collaboration.

Source: Authors' own.

- determining the faculty role and gaining commitment;
- achieving commitment from leadership from all institutional units; and
- partnering with the community (local, national, and international).

Innovation – Are We Ready?

In this step, innovation, acting upon the data above, guides the implementation plan which will utilize human, social, and financial capital. To accomplish this, it is essential to answer a few questions.

WHAT TYPE OF INNOVATION IS BEING PROPOSED?

Innovation can be incremental (Le et al., 2020; Lei et al., 2019; Torugsa et al., 2016), radical (Le et al., 2020; Lei et al., 2019), transformative

(Torugsa et al., 2016), transformational (Denning, 2005), or breakthrough (Satell, 2017). In an interview, Antoine Perruchoud, Director of the Master of Advanced Studies (MAS) program, shares "the disruption it (TA framework) brings to the teaching of entrepreneurship, as well as the perspectives opened up by this new way of teaching in different fields of business administration" (Claivaz, 2019). Determining the type of innovation is important as it provides insights into the approach of the implementation plan. The original intent of t.e.a.m. was an incremental change in the modality (delivery) of entrepreneurship studies. Since then, COVID-19 restrictions and mandates from the Board of Trustees to *reimagine* all programs and services on campus shifted the type of innovation to become a breakthrough. The problem was clearly defined; however, the need to cross domains (Satell, 2017) into other units (online vs. campus), disciplines, and modalities provided greater insights into the impact of t.e.a.m. as a breakthrough innovation.

HOW HAS THE COLLECTED KNOWLEDGE BEEN SHARED?

Creating and delivering effective and efficient communication between all stakeholders (see Figure 4.1) distributed via various channels decreased resistance and ambiguity. Conveying the collected knowledge empowered stakeholders, improved awareness on the innovation, and fostered learning.

HOW WILL THE INNOVATION BE DEPLOYED?

Taking inventory of available and needed resources and infrastructures (space, systems, technologies, budget, training, etc.), as well as determining the internal and external support systems, is required in the successful deployment of the innovation. Observing red flags, obstacles, and reasons to delay the launch is essential to identify alternative plans and exit strategies. A potential failure does not equal a loss; it equals a gain in information and learning. Innovation in the long term requires adapting a failing forward mindset, which serves as a model for future learners and entrepreneurs. An additional consideration is to determine if this is a full or a beta launch. For SNHU, this is a full launch showing a high rate of retention, access to business mentors, and seed money, an evolving community of learning.

By considering all the above, the six points to be reflected in the successful implementation of the innovation include:

- affordability for the learner and institution;
- interoperability across all units;
- scalability of programs;

- inclusivity of and equity for all prospective learners;
- desirability of programs by learners; and
- adaptability into other disciplines.

Conclusion

The challenge facing HEIs is to drastically change its delivery model/ landscape and explore how traditional campus-based institutions can best utilize technology and methodologies to achieve an engaging student experience. As Patnaik (2020) said, "More fundamentally, COVID-19 is challenging deep-rooted notions of when, where, and how we deliver education, of the role of colleges and universities, the importance of life-long learning, and the distinction we draw between traditional and non-traditional learners." This further serves as a catalyst to launch innovative learning modalities at HEIs.

Fostering innovation and transferring knowledge require strong community engagement and collaborative opportunities across all units. The feedback received from the community was an overwhelming excitement by faculty (many already want to teach with non-traditional pedagogy), a strong connection with our students (research on experiential learning vs. lecture-based learning), and a high level of engagement from faculty and staff across campus. Throughout the innovation process, practices of communication, collaboration, appreciation, recognition, reflection, resilience, and fostering a growth mindset have been fundamental to ensure the successful implementation of the BS.ENT degree using the t.e.a.m. at SNHU.

The results of the learning journey that started in 2018 have clearly outlined a viable direction for the School of Business and potentially other SNHU units. Therefore, the recommendation is to launch the BS.ENT program to provide our learners with experiences that will prepare them to become resilient contributors in their communities.

Note

1. https://akatemia.org.uk/applying-team-mastery-in-the-community/ – The Team Coach Development Programme provided support and training to the team of coaches involved in the Bachelor of Science in Entrepreneurship degree.

References

Abrams, R. M. (2017). *Entrepreneurship: A real-world approach: Hands-on guide for today's entrepreneur*. Planning Shop.

Albertsen, L., Wiedmann, K. P., & Schmidt, S. (2020). The impact of innovation-related perception on consumer acceptance of food innovations – Development of an integrated framework of the consumer acceptance process. *Food Quality and Reference, 84.* http://doi.org/10.1016/j.foodqual.2020.103958

Amabile, T. (1996). *Creativity in context: Update to "The social psychology of creativity."* Westview Press.

Anders, B. (2019). *The army learning concept, army learning model: A guide to understanding and implementation.* Sovorel Publishing.

Aragon, R., Basson, J., Burton, A., Schneider, J., Yang, W., Holman, R., & Downing, G. J. (2017). Impact of innovation initiatives in a federal government agency: Measuring and understanding the influence of culture and employee attitudes. *Innovation Journal, 22*(1), 1–51.

Baggen, Y., Minert, J., Lans, T., Biemans, H., Greiff, S., & Mulder, M. (2015). Linking complex problem solving to opportunity identification competence within the context of entrepreneurship. *International Journal of Lifelong Education, 34*(4), 412–429. http://doi.org/10.1080/02601370.2015.1060029

Barringer, B. R. (2015). *Preparing effective business plans* (2nd ed.). Pearson Education.

Bloom, J. L., & McClellan, J. L. (2016). Appreciative administration: Applying the appreciative education framework to leadership practices in higher education. *Journal of Higher Education Management, 31*(1), 195–210.

Bolland, A. (2020). Personal communication. 11th April 2020.

Chan, J., Dow, S. P., & Schunn, C. D. (2015). Do the best design ideas (really) come from conceptually distant sources of inspiration? *Design Studies, 36,* 31–58. http://doi.org/10.1016/j.destud.2014.08.001

Claivaz, D. (2019, November 5). Team Academy, the hands-on bachelor that disrupts education with Antoine Perruchoud. *Edupreneurial Pivot.* https://edupreneurial-pivot.com/en/2019/11/05/team-academy-the-hands-on-bachelor-that-disrupts-education-antoine-perruchoud/

Crilly, N., & Cardoso, C. (2017). Where next for research on fixation, inspiration, and creativity in design? *Design Studies, 50,* 1–38. http://doi.org/10.1016/j.destud. 2017.02.001

Denning, S. (2005). Transformational innovation: A journey by narrative. *Strategy & Leadership, 33*(3), 11–16. http://doi.org/10.1108/10878570510700119

Edelbroek, R., Peters, P., & Jan Blomme, R. (2019). Engaging in open innovation: The mediating role of work engagement in the relationship between transformational and transactional leadership and the quality of the open innovation process as perceived by employee. *Journal of General Management, 45*(1), 5–17. http://doi.org/10.1177/0306307019844633

Feng, C., Huang, X., & Zhang, L. (2016). A multilevel study of transformational leadership, dual organizational change, and innovative behavior in groups. *Journal of Organizational Change Management, 29*(6), 855–877. http://doi.org/10.1108/JOCM-01-2016-0005

Fowle, M., & Jussila, N. (2016, January). The adoption of a Finnish Learning Model in the UK. In *Proceedings of the European Conference on Innovation & Entrepreneurship* (pp. 194–201). Retrieved on September 25, 2020, from www.researchgate.net/publication/318214562_Team_Academy_The_Adoption_of_a_Finnish_Learning_Model_in_the_UK

Glor, E. D. (2014). Studying the impact of innovation on organizations, organizational populations and organizational communities: A framework for research. *The Innovation Journal: The Public Sector Innovation Journal, 19*(3), 1–20.

Hansen, J., Jensen, A., & Nguyen, N. (2019). The responsible learning organization can Senge (1990) teach organizations how to become responsible innovators? *The Learning Organization, 27*(1), 65–74. https://doi.org/10.1108/TLO-11-2019-0164

Hart, D. (2003). *Entrepreneurship policy: What it is and where it came from?* Cambridge University Press.

Huang, Z., Ahmed, C., & Mickael, G. (2020). A model for supporting the ideas screening during front end of the innovation process based on combination of methods of EcaTRIZ, AHP, and SWOT. *Concurrent Engineering-Research and Applications, 28*(2), 89–96. http://doi.org/10.1177/1063293X20911165

Inno-Zone. (2021). *The Innovation Dice™*. www.thediscoverycompany.nl/

Jacob, W. J., & Gokbel, V. (2018). Global higher education learning outcomes and financial trends: Comparative and innovative approaches. *International Journal of Educational Development, 58*, 5–17. http://doi.org/10.1016/j.ijedudev.2017.03.001

Kelley, T., & Kelley, D. (2013). *Creative confidence* (1st ed.). Crown Business.

Le, P. B., Lei, H., Le, T. T., Gong, J., & Ha, A. T. (2020). Developing a collaborative culture for radical and incremental innovation: The mediating roles of tacit and explicit knowledge sharing. *Chinese Management Studies, 14*(4), 957–975. http://doi.org/10.1108/CMS-04-2019-0151

LeBlanc, P. J. (2018). Higher education in a VUCA world. *Change, 50*(3–4), 23–26. https://doi.org/10.1080/00091383.2018.1507370

Lei, H., Ha, A. T., & Le, P. B. (2019). How ethical leadership cultivates radical and incremental innovation: The mediating role of tacit and explicit knowledge sharing. *Journal of Business & Industrial Marketing, 35*(5), 849–862. http://doi.org/10.1108/JBIM-05-2019-0180

Medeiros, K. E., Steele, L. M., Watts, L. L., & Mumford, M. D. (2018). Timing is everything: Examining the role of constraints throughout the creative process. *Psychology of Aesthetics Creativity and the Arts, 12*(4), 471–488. http://doi.org/10.1037/aca0000148

Mumford, M. D., Mobley, M. I., Reiter-Palmon, R., Uhlman, C. E., & Doares, L. M. (1991). Process analytic models of creative capacities. *Creativity Research Journal, 4*, 91–122. http://doi.org/10.1080/10400419109534380

Mwasalwiba, E. (2010). Entrepreneurship education: A review of its objectives, teaching methods, and impact indicators. *Education and Training, 52*(1), 20–47. http://doi.org/10.1108/00400911011017663

Patnaik, J. (2020, July 5). Transformation of higher education: How COVID-19 is changing the face of education. *Business World*. http://bweducation.businessworld.in/article/Transformation-Of-Higher-Education-How-COVID-19-Is-Changing-The-Face-Of-Education/08-07-2020-295372/

Price, R., & Wrigley, C. (2016). Design and a deep customer insight approach to innovation. *Journal of International Consumer Marketing, 28*(2), 92–105. http://doi.org/10.1080/08961530.2015.1092405

Ruuska, J., & Krawczyk, P. (2013). Team Academy as learning living lab. Conference Paper on *European Phenomena of Entrepreneurship Education and Development*. University Industry Conference, 27–29 May 2013, Amsterdam, NL.

Satell, G. (2017). The 4 types of innovation and the problems they solve. *Harvard Business Review*. https://hbr.org/2017/06/the-4-types-of-innovation-and-the-problems-they-solve

Senge, P. M. (1990). *The fifth discipline: The art and practice of the learning organization*. Doubleday/Currency.

Seonghoon, B., Shengen, L., Byungjoo, L., & Kwangyun, W. (2018). Closing the loop of inspiration-to-creation: Responding with programmable sphere. *Leonardo*, *51*(3), 280–281. http://doi.org/10.1162/LEON_a_01598

Sio, U. N., Kotovshy, K., & Cagan, J. (2015). Fixation or inspiration? A meta-analytic review of the role of examples on design processes. *Design Studies*, *39*, 70–99. http://doi.org/10.1016/j.destud.2015.04.004

Sirelkhatim, F., & Gangi, Y. (2015). Entrepreneurship education: A systematic literature review of curricula contents and teaching methods. *Cogent Business & Management*, *2*(1), 1052034. http://doi.org/10.1080/23311975.2015.1052034

Torugsa, N., & Wayne, O'D. (2016). Progress in innovation and knowledge management research: From incremental to transformative innovation. *Journal of Business Research*, *69*(5), 1610–1614. http://doi.org/10.1016/j.jbusres.2015.10.026

Tosey, P., Dhaliwal, S., & Hassinen, J. (2015). The Finnish Team Academy model: Implications for management education. *Management Learning*, *46*(2), 175–194. http://doi.org/10.1177/1350507613498334

Treffinger, D. J., & Isaksen, S. G. (1992). *Creative problem solving: An introduction*. Center for Creative Learning.

Working to learn. (2020). https://akatemia.org.uk/

5   The Joyous Envy of Seeing Real Action Experienced and Reflected Upon

Colin Jones

Introduction

As the provision of entrepreneurship education (EE) increases globally, there have been increasing calls to use reflective thinking to counterbalance the use of action-oriented experiential forms of learning in EE (Hägg, 2017). However, despite empirical and conceptual work outlining the importance and process of reflection in EE (Jones, 2009, 2011; Neck et al., 2014), there is little evidence of the widespread, effective use of critical reflection in EE. This chapter aims to address this issue through highlighting the presence of reflective practice deemed to be excellent in the context of contemporary EE, as reconciled to the extant literature on reflection and transformative learning (Mezirow, 1978; Cagney, 2014; Doris, 2015). The remainder of this chapter is structured as follows. First, a description of the author's ideas on what constitutes the context of contemporary EE are presented. Second, several problems related to agency, reflection, and value creation, in the context of contemporary EE, are discussed. Third, the author's observations of the nature of student learning occurring from engagement with the Team Academy (TA) model (Leinonen et al., 2004) of EE are presented. Finally, several conclusions are drawn from the discussions presented, with implications outlined for both the TA approach and EE more generally.

Contemporary Entrepreneurship Education

As the 21st century unfolds, EE is increasingly positioned within the higher education landscape globally as education (in a narrow sense) for new venture creation and education (in a broader sense) for the development of essential employability skills (Ustav & Venesaar, 2018). Drawing upon Barnett's (2004) concerns for developing graduate students for an uncertain world, Jones et al. (2019) argue for an even broader role for EE, one related to developing reflective and thoughtful graduates capable of advanced levels

DOI: 10.4324/9781003163091-6

of sense making. Such thinking places great importance upon the locus of student needs, bringing additional focus upon the balance between each individual student's general and immediate needs (Tyler, 1949). Viewed from this perspective, the use of student-oriented heutagogical and andragogical methods (Jones et al., 2014) complement the educator's pedagogical practices to ensure the self-determined learning opportunities of individual students are adequately supported. Thus, first, EE is directed at the fabric of each student's current life, and second, at developing the prerequisite skills and mindset required to underwrite the agency for future self-directed action (Jones, 2019). In this context, EE quickly has become many things to many people, commonly infused into education in the arts, the sciences, and the social sciences and commonly focused on commerce and industry. There are two interrelated processes that are commonly assumed to support the transformative nature of learning in EE, those being critical reflection and value creation. We will now briefly consider the role and challenges of each process within this context of EE.

Viewed in the simplest way, students of EE are assumed to develop a capacity for entrepreneurial agency through experiential learning that is often aligned to attempts to create forms of value. The issue of whom should gain from such value creation remains a contested issue (Jones et al., 2019), but regardless, value creation remains a central organizing feature of EE.

Reflection

The process of reflection is assumed to be present within the process of EE given the prevalence of action-oriented (Hägg, 2017) practices. The importance attributed to reflection in the learning process has long been recognized (Dewey, 1910), but is not always assumed to be simplistic in operation (Beard & Wilson, 2002). While the logic of Kolb's (1984) approach, exploiting a dialectic tension to support reflection upon concrete experiences, in order to make sense of such experience, is not disputed, the efficacy of such a learning process is often questioned. For example, Miettinen (2000) discusses the problem of contemporary scholars (e.g. Kolb) implicitly assuming that meaningful reflection is likely to occur after we experience events. Referring directly to Dewey's concern of the dominance of (subconscious) human habits overriding our conscious habits, it is more likely that the automatic pilot (Beard & Wilson, 2002) mode of operation that is present in our day-to-day lives will often block meaningful reflection on our daily experiences. Put simply, assuming that the learning process can be aligned sequentially to activity cycles (i.e. experiencing, interpreting, generalizing, and applying) gives humans more control over their cognitive abilities than is observed in reality. All of these cast a shadow of doubt over one of the most assumed mechanisms of learning in EE.

The broader implications of such concerns are explored in greater detail by Doris (2015, p. X) where the accuracy of human reflection is considered: "The exercise of human agency consists in judgement and *behavior* ordered by self-conscious reflection about what to think and do. Typically, this doctrine is associated with a corollary: the exercise of human agency requires accurate reflection." This issue of accuracy is rarely discussed in the EE literature, with the premise seemingly being that all methods of reflection practice will enhance student learning outcomes. From the perspective of Doris, this is simply not so, because quality will always trump quantity. This is not a new idea, since Plato, the importance of accurate self-understanding has been aligned to notions of practical wisdom (or phronesis), where an individual is able to locate "the prudent course of action and resist the urgings of the passions and the deceptions of the senses" (Robinson, 1990, p. 14). So, while it is easy to find agreement as to the importance of developing entrepreneurial agency in EE, little consensus exists around how precisely this should be done.

The earlier works of Jung (1921) spoke of personal development through a process of individuation or self-differentiation. Through the process of individuation, higher degrees of critical reflection pave the way for individuals to choose a preferred life pathway. Such lofty outcomes are implicitly embedded in EE, where assumptions abound about graduates taking control of their lives and marshalling the resources at their disposal to create and capture value. However, achieving the required "fidelity to the law of one's own being" (Cranton, 2000, p. 189) requires "the segregation of the individual from the undifferentiated and unconscious herd," or isolation, something rarely pedagogically prescribed. So, a conundrum seems to exist in EE, and most obviously also in other disciplines, that being that challenge of supporting students to engage in sufficient (accurate) critical reflection, so as to enable well-directed entrepreneurial agency to be developed. This requires a heightened capacity for both introspection and extrospection (Doris, 2015) to ensure sufficient awareness of not only oneself but also others and surrounds. While there are a few exceptions (see Jones, 2009, 2011), the development of reflection of others and surrounds has not been the central focus of reflective practice in EE. Doris contends that human agency is more likely to be fuelled by ignorance and self-deception. That is, it is easier to assume we have developed self-awareness when in reality all that may have been developed is self-ignorance.

Such thinking echoes the insights of Sumner (1902, p. 67) who posited that:

> [T]he observation that the motives and purposes have nothing to do with consequences is a criterion for distinguishing between the science of society and the views, whims, ideals, and fads which are current in regard to social matters, but especially for distinguishing between socialism and sociology. Motives and purposes are in the brain and heart of man. Consequences are in the world of fact. The former is infected by human ignorance, folly, self-deception, and passion; the latter are sequences of cause and effect dependent upon the nature of the forces at work.

When applying such sentiments to EE, the vital role of accurate critical reflection becomes very clear. The development of agency requires, on the part of the student, four distinct behaviours (Bandura, 2006). First, a demonstration of *intentionality* (or purpose) in order to advance their own desires. Second, the related process of *forethought* introduces a temporal component to the student's thinking, enabling their imagination to play forward alongside their purpose and visualize what might be possible. Third, students must use *self-reactiveness* to self-assess their current abilities and assumed potentiality vis-à-vis their developing purpose. Fourth, Bandura highlights the importance of *self-reflectiveness* to ensure a student has adequate metacognitive abilities to recognise the soundness of their thinking.

It is in this demanding context that transformative learning (Mezirow, 1978) is increasingly purported to drive EE learning outcomes. However, it would seem that many educators in the domain are increasingly agnostic regarding the likelihood of students reflecting with sufficient accuracy to ensure the seeds of profitable agency are being sown. There are two reasons why such cynicism may be present. First, EE either is often positioned around the development of formulaic business plans (completed with relatively untested assumptions) about fanciful futuristic business ventures or remains tethered to texts and theory bases and the subsequent testing of the memorization of such theories. Second, the educational process is typically devoid of an authentic disconcerting dilemma (Mezirow, 2000; Cagney, 2014) through which the student's internal bearings are disoriented. The work of Kember et al. (2008) provides signposts that can be used to reconcile student attempts to reflect into categories ranging from non-reflective, to understanding, to reflection, to critical reflection. Despite eternal confidence globally that EE equates to a transformational learning journey for many students, the jury would seem yet to have returned a verdict upon the presence of accurate reflection underpinning the development of agency in EE.

Value Creation

The second key aspect of EE is that of value creation, which students are assumed to develop a capacity for. There are those (Lackéus, 2019) that assume that students develop valuable entrepreneurial competencies through engaging in value creation processes, while others (Jones et al., 2021) hold that significant reflection upon one's life purpose is required to develop the entrepreneurial agency needed for authentic value creation. In this chapter, the semantics of such opposing views will be sidestepped in order to remain focused on the role of reflection in EE. Nevertheless, a key issue in positioning the process of value creation in EE is appreciating the extent to which students are acting on their general or immediate needs (Tyler, 1949) when engaging with value creation activities. Value creation being defined here as the "difference between use and exchange value" as contemplated across "all levels of analysis" (Lepak et al., 2007, p. 190), *uses* referring to the potential satisfaction one gains from the use of their (existing and developing) knowledge, skills, and/or capabilities, and *exchanges* referring to what can be obtained through the exchange of one's knowledge, skills, and/or capabilities (Jones et al., 2021).

Consistent with the first-documented value creation pedagogy of Tsunesaburo Makiguchi (Bethel, 1989) nearly 100 years ago, and notions of creating reasonable adventurers (Heath, 1964; Jones, 2007), enabling students to introduce the raw ingredients of their lives, acting on their individual immediate needs and developing the ability to reflect deeply, should all be prerequisite inputs for value creation activities. So, it is the growth of students that is the stimulus for increasing agency and thereby supporting a capacity for self-directed action. In the context of EE, Jones et al. (2021) offered a visualization of the perfect student's development. Ideally, students would be given an opportunity to explore their sense of self in order to develop a sense of purpose. Barnett (2007) speaks of the need for students to embrace the challenges of an educational voyage. A process of ontological discomfort through which self-travel is of more importance than intellectual travel. Therefore, it is argued that through such personal discovery, deep skills in reflection can be developed, skills that feed into the capacity for human agency (Bandura, 2006), and thus, the ability to profitably create value for one's self and others. The remaining sections of this chapter introduce a unique EE context and the author's observations of student behaviour in that context, before concluding remarks are presented.

Team Academy

The TA approach to EE, which was developed in Finland around 30 years ago, has been credited with producing increased levels of graduate self-awareness (Ruuska & Krawczyk, 2013). Hatt (2021) notes that the TA approach, in comparison to more traditional approaches, is a different way of structuring and delivering EE, with little defined content knowledge, preferring instead to focus on the immediate needs using a coaching methodology. The author observed the TA approach at two English universities. Of particular interest was the extent to which the coaching pedagogy actually puts the student in control of their development of knowledge and skills as they facilitate their own experiential learning process.

On Reflection

In general, EE can be a difficult subject area for students for a variety of reasons. For some, the action-oriented focus can be very confronting, producing anxiety and other performance related fears. Coupled with the need to then reflect on such action, many students find the tempo and requirements of EE to be too great a departure from other subject areas in which a more passive orientation to learning is the norm. Conversely, for other students of EE, there is too much distance between the curriculum requirements and their own individual needs, vis-à-vis taking action on ideas and/or solving the problems of their lives. Finally, the lack of structure around theories or the neat progression from concept to concept can also unsettle those that seek to retain control over their learning journeys. To the outsider looking in, the TA approach provides little refuge for the traditional student, and this is what makes it and the students' learning journeys so entrepreneurial.

Dewey (1913, p. 2) famously argued that the "theory of effort simply substitutes one interest for another," and in the context of the TA approach, student effort is maximized by authentically aligning the student's learning context to their life's context: a rare educational occurrence in higher education. Interacting with the TA students as an observer, a presenter and mentor produced many moments of reflection. It was very clear that at every stage of the course, the students were engaged as learners in ways that change their life. They were invested in ways unlike most students who tend to look at their subjects, keeping their personal lives separate. Through this integrated approach, reflection was meaningful in that it *mattered*. As the dynamics of the student groups developed, in terms of interpersonal relationships, it was clear that the process of thinking was slowed due to a heightened concern for one another's' feelings. As a result, their reflection was able to flourish within a gap that was often present between stimulus and response. This *stop* in thinking (Appelbaum, 1995) appeared to inject both time and depth into the process of reflection, with the identities of the individual students very much in play. Having not observed this dynamic in student interaction in EE previously, I initially lost sight of the contribution of the TA approach to entrepreneurship. However, once the obvious nature of student development was recognized, the direct links to EE also became obvious.

Through my conversations with the students, both collectively and individually, it was apparent that they found the TA process very difficult, very confronting, and yet vitally important to their development. Thinking back to the nature of Mezirow's transformative learning (Cagney, 2014) for the students, in varying degrees, all experienced some form of a disorienting dilemma. The vulnerability and eventual trust required to maintain each of the student groups challenged each individual's well-being. Next, it was very clear that the students were forced to examine their personal assumptions and beliefs in order to help develop and enact the group's objectives. Further, there was evidence the students were required to reframe their conception of reality. Finally, as per Jung's (1921) process of individuation, the students spoke of the new perspectives developed as a result of group interaction that were increasingly underwriting their group's progress. In summary, the TA approach directly shapes students more so than it does entrepreneurial ventures. Yet, it develops students in such a fundamental way that their authentic potential to develop entrepreneurial agency is enhanced, vis-à-vis more traditional approaches to EE. Put simply, TA is an entrepreneurial theatre within which a student development play occurs.

Conclusions

TA is unique, and it elevates student development over project development, despite their interrelatedness. Indeed, project success is dependent upon the collective development of the student group. It was very clear that the quality of coaching provided by educators is critically important to supporting appropriate student development. In the absence of a specified curriculum, it is the students' immediate needs that are the central guiding element of the students' development. In contrast to traditional EE programs, the implicit learning outcomes (entrepreneurial agency) are developed through an explicit focus on student development. A consequence of this approach is the time and expert support given to the process of critical reflection. This vital capability in the process of human agency is fully supported in the TA approach. It is as if the actor's script has been downplayed, while the actor's ability to read, memorize, interpret, and deliver the script's lines is revered. While the script can be rewritten and/ or substituted for alternative scripts, but the underlying ability of the actor remains of central importance.

The obvious challenge for the TA approach is three-fold. First, the approach is very intensive in terms of the student to educator ratio, something that goes against the trends in contemporary higher education. Second, the nature of the coaching expertise observed is not part of the educator's traditional skill set, especially in business faculties where EE is often hosted. Third, student awareness (and/or appreciation) of the TA approach is a multifaceted problem. On the one hand, student enrolments are needed to maintain economic viability. On the other hand, too many enrolments would most likely impinge upon the space required for students to discover themselves and the new roles they are capable of performing.

Conversely, traditional EE programs seem to be missing a trick when it comes to supporting authentic critical reflection. Through packing curriculums with either too much content and/or experiential learning opportunities, both of which are often starved of authentic critical reflection. An invisible paradox appears to be ever present in EE, one between naïve optimism and realism. The optimism inherent within most student business plans far outweighs the realism of unknown realities. And yet, transformative learning is often very challenging, incorporating grief, pain, and conflict (Cranton, 2016), all vital inputs to enable "a structural reorganization in the way a person looks at" themselves and their relationships with others and environs (Mezirow, 1978, p. 108). This suggests an opportunity exists to embrace the deeper style of learning in EE.

Palmer (1998) refers to the hidden wholeness that often remains dormant between paradoxical poles. There is always the potential of mistakenly arguing for a neglected dimension, such as critical reflection, and then over-correcting in our response. The challenge being to avoid *either/or* situations, instead, seeking to think about the world together. Without doubt, there is a joyous envy of seeing real entrepreneurial action experienced and reflected upon. The recent reworks of Jones et al. (2014) and Jones et al. (2019) outline a pathway towards uniting optimism and realism through the adoption of heutagogical methods. Once the immediate needs (Tyler, 1949) of each individual student become the context of each student's learning, then the optimism of the naïve can be balanced against a reality that can be more readily appreciated via authentic critical reflection. Perhaps the most important step that EE needs to take is the initial substitution of business contexts for life contexts. Only then can fanciful optimism be tamed by the reality of life's harsh lessons.

References

Appelbaum, D. (1995). *The stop*. State University of New York Press.

Bandura, A. (2006). Towards a psychology of human agency. *Perspectives on Psychological Science, 1*(2), 164–180.

Barnett, R. (2004). Learning for an unknown future. *Higher Education Research & Development, 23*(3), 247–260.

Barnett, R. (2007). *A will to learn: Being a student in an age of uncertainty*. McGraw Hill.

Beard, C., & Wilson, J. (2002). *Experiential learning*. Kogan.

Bethel, D. (1989). *Education for creative living: Ideas and proposals of Tsunesaburo Makiguchi*. Iowa State University Press.

Cagney, A. (2014). Transformative learning. In D. Coghlan & M. Brydon-Miller (Eds.), *The SAGE encyclopedia of action research*. Sage Publications.

Cranton, P. (2000). Individual differences and transformative learning. In J. Mezirow (Ed.), *Learning as transformation: Critical perspectives on a theory in progress*. Jossey-Bass Publishers.

Cranton, P. (2016). *Understanding and promoting transformative learning: A guide to theory and practice*. Stylus Publishing.

Dewey, J. (1910). *How we think*. D.C. Heath.

Dewey, J. (1913). *Interest and effort in education*. Houghton Mifflin Company.

Doris, J. (2015). *Talking to ourselves*. Oxford University Press.

Hägg, G. (2017). *Experiential entrepreneurship education: Reflective thinking as a counterbalance to action for developing entrepreneurial knowledge* (Doctoral thesis, Lund University). MediaTry ck. https://portal.research.lu.se/portal/en/publications/experiential-entrepreneurship-education(16e94e4d-f523-4b5e-8557-2263b77be867).html

Hatt, L. (2021). Learning enterprise and entrepreneurship through real business projects. In D. Morley & M. Jamil (Eds.), *Applied pedagogies for higher education*. Palgrave Macmillan.

Heath, R. (1964). *The reasonable adventurer*. University of Pittsburgh Press.

Jones, C. (2007). Creating the reasonable adventurer: The co-evolution of student and learning environment. *Journal of Small Business and Enterprise Development, 14*(2), 228–240.

Jones, C. (2009). Enterprise education: Learning through personal experience. *Industry and Higher Education, 23*(3), 175–182.

Jones, C. (2011). *Teaching entrepreneurship to undergraduates*. Edward Elgar Publishing.

Jones, C. (2019). *How to teach entrepreneurship*. Edward Elgar Publishing.

Jones, C., Matlay, H., Penaluna, K., & Penaluna, A. (2014). Claiming the future of enterprise education. *Education + Training, 56*(8–9), 764–775.

Jones, C., Penaluna, K., & Penaluna, A. (2019). The promise of andragogy, heutagogy and academagogy to enterprise and entrepreneurship education pedagogy. *Education + Training, 61*(9), 1170–1186.

Jones, C., Penaluna, A., and Penaluna, K. (2021). Value creation in entrepreneurial education: Towards a unified approach. *Education and Training, 63*(1), 101–113.

Jung, C. (1921). *Personality types*. Bollinger Press.

Kember, D., McKay, J., Sinclair, K., & Wong, F. (2008). A four category scheme for coding and assessing the level of reflection in written work. *Assessment & Evaluation in Higher Education, 33*(4), 369–379.

Kolb, D. (1984). *Experiential learning: Experience as the source of learning and development*. Englewood Cliffs, NJ: Prentice Hall.

Lackéus, M. (2019). Making enterprise education more relevant through mission creep. In G. Mulholland & J. Turner (Eds.), *Enterprising education in UK higher education: Challenges for theory and practice*. Routledge.

Leinonen, N., Partanen, J., & Palviainen, P. (2004). *Team Academy: A true story of a community that learns by doing*. PS-kustannnus, Jyväskylä.

Lepak, D., Smith, K., & Taylor, S. (2007). Value creation and value capture: A multilevel perspective. *Academy of Management Review, 32*(1), 180–194.

Mezirow, J. (1978). Perspective transformation. *Adult Education, 28*(2), 100–110.

Mezirow, J. (2000). *Learning as transformation: Critical perspectives on a theory in progress*. Jossey Bass.

Miettinen, R. (2000). The concept of experiential learning and John Dewey's theory of reflective thought and action. *International Journal of Lifelong Education, 19*(1), 54–72.

Neck, H., Greene, P., & Brush, C. (2014). *Teaching entrepreneurship: A practice-based approach*. Edward Elgar Publishing.

Palmer, P. (1998). *The courage to teach*. Jossey-Bass.

Robinson, D. (1990). Wisdom through the ages. In R. Sternberg (Ed.), *Wisdom: Its nature, origins, and development*. Cambridge University Press.

Ruuska, J., & Krawczyk, P. (2013). *Team academy as learning living lab* [Paper presentation]. University Industry Conference, Amsterdam.

Sumner, W. (1902). *Earth-hunger and other essays*. Yale University Press.

Tyler, R. (1949). *Basic principles of curriculum and instruction*. University of Chicago Press.

Ustav, S., & Venesaar, U. (2018). Bridging metacompetencies and entrepreneurship education. *Education + Training, 60*(7–8), 674–695.

6 Entrepreneurship Education in the United Kingdom

Traditional Teacher-Led Learning Approaches Versus the Experiential Team Academy Model

Isaac Oduro Amoako, Gideon Maas, and Kwame Oduro Amoako

Introduction

The field of EE has been characterized by explosive growth given the importance of entrepreneurship in job and wealth creation (Koellinger & Thurik, 2012; Lumpkin & Bacq, 2019). Not surprisingly, across the globe, entrepreneurship is taught to students at different levels and across many different disciplines (Jones & Iredale, 2006). For example, in the United States, entrepreneurship courses increased ten-fold between 1979 and 2001 (Katz, 2003). Yet, entrepreneurship courses may not necessarily lead to jobs and wealth creation due to the aims of the course and how it is taught and learned. Entrepreneurship involves opportunity recognition, market knowledge, and experience in a given context, and these are subjective and socially constructed (Shane & Venkataraman, 2000; Chell, 2007; Malmström et al., 2017; Amoako, 2019), and hence, entrepreneurship knowledge should be co-created with learners. Yet, studies show that most entrepreneurship courses in higher education and particularly universities across the world predominantly use traditional classroom teacher-led approaches that focus on the transmission and reproduction of knowledge, telling students what to observe and read while paying less attention to the experiences of the learners and what they can do (see Hytti & O'Gorman, 2004; Matlay & Mitchell, 2006). However, given the subjective and experiential nature of entrepreneurship, the traditional methods are not effective in fostering the required practical competencies. This explains why entrepreneurship educators, researchers, and policy makers have recently emphasized the need for

DOI: 10.4324/9781003163091-7

instructors to shift from teacher-led approaches to contemporary methods that emphasise experience, acting in the real world and reflection in order to build entrepreneurial competencies among learners (e.g. Fayolle & Toutain, 2013; QAA, 2018). Yet, there are challenges in identifying practical models by which experiential EE can be implemented in higher education.

This chapter aims to compare traditional teacher-led approaches with the student-centred Team Academy (TA) approach in EE focusing on the roles of the instructor and the learner. The TA model originated in Finland in 1993 when Johannes Partanen, a marketing lecturer at JAMK University of Applied Sciences in Jyvaskyla, who had become disillusioned with traditional teacher-led management education wanted students to create enterprise projects to fund their trips abroad. After his advertisement, students who enrolled on the programme successfully developed ventures to raise the needed funds for the trip. Since then, Johannes went on to develop a Bachelor of Business Administration (BBA) programme that requires students to create and run their own ventures for the three- and half-year duration of the course. His innovative experiential learning model has since trained over a thousand students, and the model has been adopted by a number of universities across the world.

The findings are used to propose a practical model that shows the five phases of learner-led entrepreneurial experiential learning (EEL) in higher education.

To achieve this, a review of the literature on teaching and learning in EE, Bloom's (1956) taxonomy and Kolb's (1984) experiential learning theory (ELT), and three case studies of entrepreneurship courses delivered in three UK universities were presented. The findings show marked dissimilarities between traditional teacher-centred entrepreneurship pedagogy compared with student-centred entrepreneurial experiential pedagogy.

We contribute to the literature in two ways. We combine the literature and empirical data to compare traditional teacher-led entrepreneurship pedagogy with experiential student-centred pedagogy to show the stark differences in course aims, role of instructor, student motivations on the course, and role of the learner. In addition, we present the EEL framework to show that experiential learning in EE is most effective when the learner has the intention to engage in concrete entrepreneurship experience, conceptual learning, reflection, and experimentation. The EEL framework can be used to effectively implement experiential entrepreneurship pedagogy in higher education.

The rest of this chapter is organized as follows: The next section presents a review of Bloom's and Kolb's learning models and teacher-led and experiential learner-centred EE. Afterwards, the methods are discussed, and the findings, discussions, and conclusions are presented. Finally, the suggestions for future research are presented.

Teacher-Led Learning Versus Experiential Learning

Bloom (1956) presented a classroom learning model that involved six stages:

1. Knowledge – behaviours that emphasize remembering or recall of ideas and phenomenon,
2. Comprehension – expectation from students when confronted with communication to know and be able to use materials or ideas communicated,
3. Application – Ability to rightly select and implement ideas without being shown how to use it in a particular situation
4. Analysis – The breakdown of materials into constituent parts and understanding of the relationships of the parts,
5. Synthesis – the putting together elements and parts so as to form the whole,
6. Evaluation – Appraising the extent to which elements are accurate, effective, economical or satisfying based on criteria as well as standards (Bloom, 1956, pp. 62–185).

Bloom's model posits that the initial stages must be followed before the learner progresses to the next stage. Hence, application and experience must follow knowledge and comprehension.

In contrast to Bloom's (1956) classroom model, Kolb (1984) identified a four-stage experiential learning model. According to Kolb (1984), learning involves

1. Experience – New concrete experience initiates the learning process,
2. Reflection – Reflection on the experience occurs from different perspectives,
3. **Concept** – Abstract conceptualizations that enable reflections to translate into logically sound theories,
4. **Experiment** – Active experimentation happens when the newly constructed theories are utilized in decision-making and problem solving.

Given the importance of concepts and theoretical knowledge in entrepreneurial learning (see Gibb, 2002) and the experiential and subjective nature of entrepreneurship (see Chell, 2007; Pittaway & Cope, 2007; European Commission, 2008), in this chapter, Bloom's (1956) and Kolb's (1984) models are utilized to conceptualise the findings from the case studies.

Entrepreneurship Education and Experiential Learning

Entrepreneurship education could focus on education *about*, *for*, and *through* entrepreneurship (Gibb, 1987; Pittaway & Edwards, 2012). *About* courses mostly focus on teaching theories of entrepreneurship and thus uses the traditional teacher-led approach of teaching and learning. *For* courses teach theories and provide practical activities that enable learners to engage with entrepreneurship. *Through* courses allow students to do what entrepreneurs do by starting real businesses or imaginary businesses through, for example, simulation. Interestingly, Pittaway and Edwards (2012) conclude that the *About* courses are the most common; however, their focus is on imparting knowledge and awareness, rather than developing *entrepreneurial skills, attitudes, and behaviours* (Pittaway & Edwards, 2012; Nabi et al., 2017). Yet, even though obtaining knowledge and awareness are important in entrepreneurship, the process involves action in starting up a business entity through the identification of opportunities in a familiar industry and a combination of information to develop a product or service that creates value for others, and in the process, they create businesses (Shane, 2000). Thus, entrepreneurship is experiential, subjective, and socially constructed (Chell, 2007). Jones et al. (2021) acknowledge that EE is not suitable for all students, but that they should be exposed to enterprising skills during their HEI programme. Such programmes require training, time, and investment with ongoing reinforcement and reinvestment.

Entrepreneurship knowledge in higher education therefore should be co-created with learners. Hence, constructivist and experiential learning approaches that enable learners to be responsible for their own learning through reflection and critical thinking could be more beneficial to learners (Kolb, 1984). Experiential learning is defined as a sequence of events which require active involvement by the student at various points (Kolb, 1984). Even though there are many different learning objectives that utilize experiential learning, the key feature of all of them is that one learns best through active involvement (Astin, 1984; Kolb, 1984). However, there are challenges in implementing EEL in higher education including the rigidity of an academic environment which might be in conflict with the complexity and variability of the entrepreneurial process, and lacking a multidisciplinary approach (Preedy et al., 2020).

We draw on the findings of this chapter to propose a model (see Figure 6.1) to show that experiential learning is more effective based on student intention to learn experientially, conceptualization, experience, reflection and application. We discuss the methods used in the next section.

Methods

This study used a literature review and three case studies from three final-year undergraduate entrepreneurship courses in three UK universities. The researchers adopted an ethno-case study approach to compare three case studies. The ethno-case study describes an inquiry concerning people that employs techniques associated with long-term and intensive ethnography but which is limited in terms of scope, time in the field, and engagement with data (Parker-Jenkins, 2018, p. 18). The amount of time spent in observing and collecting data was not long enough to warrant the method to be regarded as an ethnography research, but instead it fits the ethno-case approach.

The study was undertaken between 2013 and 2018 during which semi-structured interviews were conducted with three instructors and six final-year students on three undergraduate BA Entrepreneurship programmes in three UK universities. The nine respondents consisted of one instructor and two students of entrepreneurship in each university. The respondents were selected based on convenience sampling as they were approached during training sessions and conferences in the various universities. The data were collected through face-to-face semi-structured interviews that lasted from 40 to 60 minutes during which open questions guarded by an interview schedule was used to allow the respondents the freedom to talk and comment about things that are important and linked to the topic (Minichiello et al., 2008). In addition to the semi-structured interviews, the researcher used participant observation by attending lectures, workshops, and team meetings while studying Cases 1, 2, 3, respectively.

Thematic analysis was adopted as a framework to analyse the data. The main concepts that emerged from the interviews were identified, coded, and then categorized into common themes (Braun & Clarke, 2006). The main themes were course aims, role of instructors, intentions of learners, and role of learners. Statements and quotes allocated to the themes were then used to present a textural and structural description of the differences between teaching and learning with the student-centred TA EE model. The EEL framework was then developed from the empirical data.

Teacher-Led Versus Student-Centred Teaching and Learning Approaches in Entrepreneurship Education

This section presents the findings from the three case studies in the United Kingdom to help unravel the differences between teacher-led and student-centred learning in entrepreneurship pedagogy in higher education.

Case 1: Entrepreneurship Module

Course Aims

The course adopted the "About" approach and aimed to provide an understanding of theoretical perspectives and practices of entrepreneurship in the United Kingdom and across the world.

Role of Instructor

Staff who designed and delivered the course were recruited based on primarily a PhD qualification. The course was delivered in a classroom on a weekly one-hour lecture and two-hour seminar basis. The assessment included an individual presentation and an individual report. Each semester, the instructor invited an entrepreneur to deliver a guest lecture during one of the lectures.

Learners Intentions

Students sought to acquire a degree in entrepreneurship learning in a classroom. Hence, skills acquired included abstract conceptualization and inductive reasoning and the ability to create theoretical models, creative problem solving, teamwork, and presentations skills.

Role of Learners

In the lecture sessions, students listened to the instructor who sought to impart greater knowledge and create awareness on the importance of entrepreneurship, historic developments, theoretical developments, value systems, and enabling and inhibiting factors and practices of entrepreneurship. However, most of the students found the lectures to be quite boring, and one student commented "the lectures are important for understanding the course but they are boring" (Student 1). During the seminars, students worked in groups to do various activities such as analysing case studies and the environmental factors that enable and constrain the development of entrepreneurship.

Case 2

Course Aims

The aim of the course was to train learners to become entrepreneurial as well as entrepreneurs, and it adopted *for* approach to entrepreneurial education.

Role of Instructor

Staff who designed and delivered the course were academics with PhDs and an entrepreneurial background. The course was delivered on a weekly one-hour lecture and three-hour workshop basis. During week 3, the instructor provided £1.00 to each team of four to five students in the workshop group as seed capital for a three-week trading activity. Furthermore, the instructor acted as a facilitator and provided introductory letters to students prior to the three-week trading. The assessments included an individual reflective journal, a group business plan presentation, and a group business plan report. During students' presentations, the instructor invited an entrepreneur to serve as a panel member to provide practical feedback to enable students develop their businesses further.

Learners Intentions

Students on the programme were recruited via A level results, and they sought to acquire a degree in Business Management. The core skills developed by learners included abstract conceptualization and inductive reasoning and problem solving. In addition, the three-week trading activity enabled learners to gain entrepreneurship experiences and acquire skills such as opportunity recognition, ideation, start-up, teamwork, networking, presentation, and personal development albeit for only three weeks. However, while some students who had intentions to be entrepreneurial or become entrepreneurs liked the trading activity, others focus were on the acquisition of knowledge and a degree disliked it.

Role of Learners

Learners on the programme attended a weekly one-hour lecture and three-hour workshop during the semester. Students in teams of fours and fives traded with their £1.00 seed capital for three weeks. The process involved idea generation and building a company (albeit unregistered) to trade with the £1.00 during workshop hours. At the end of the semester, the student group that made the highest profits was awarded a prize. While some students liked the practical trading experiences, others loathed it. Two students expressed it in this way; "I like the trading weeks because they enable me to practice what I have been taught during the lectures, the only problem is that the time is too short to learn how to start a business properly" (Student 1). Student 2 disagreed: "the three weeks has been wasted, I came to uni to learn but not to trade." Students were required to write a reflexive journal about their trading experiences, and the journal formed part of the assessments.

Case 3: Team Academy Model

Course Aims

This course adopted the "through" approach based on the TA model that aims to create real-world experiences through "learning-by-doing," to enable learners to become entrepreneurs and/or agile and commercially minded entrepreneurial individuals that organizations need.

Role of Instructor

The instructor on the course was an academic and an experienced entrepreneur with industry experience and vital industry links and networks. Before the commencement of the course, she visited other universities that used the TA model in the United Kingdom and abroad to learn about TA philosophy, experiential teaching and learning, coaching course content, and how to design learning outcomes and course content. At the beginning of the academic year, the instructor set the parameters with everything that learners needed to know. However, the instructor did not determine the weekly schedule and when learners should achieve the learning. Instead, she informed learners that responsibility for learning was theirs, and all learning and trading activities should comply with university regulation. Even though the assessments were written by the instructor, the students were asked to rewrite them. During the weekly team meetings, the instructor served as a coach and therefore facilitated learning by checking what learners were doing and supporting and challenging them when necessary. The instructor commented on the strengths and weaknesses of the course in this way: "Our course ensures that learners learn by doing in order to become the kind of agile and commercially minded entrepreneurs and intrapreneurs that organizations are crying out for; the main challenge of this model is the lack of theoretical knowledge."

Learners' Intentions

Learners on the course were recruited based on A levels and an interview that ascertained whether the student had the motivation to embark on an experiential learning journey. Learners' who had intentions to acquire a range of hands-on entrepreneurial experiences and competencies including skills in opportunity recognition, ideation, start-up, management of the survival, and growth stages of a venture were recruited after the interview.

Role of Learners

Learners on the course were in teams that were formed at the beginning of the course. Each team had three 3-hour team meetings with a coach each week in a space that formed part of the teaching facilities but did not look like a standard classroom. The teams took ownership of the space to some extent, and access was limited to normal university hours although teams were usually on-site for most of the day. All learning was focused around team projects as there were no formal classroom delivery. Learners were thus in charge of their own learning including inviting entrepreneurs guest speakers to give talks to them. A second-year student commented that "in this course students take it upon themselves but the model will not work for everyone but for those who have a passion to do entrepreneurship and I will recommend it to someone who is entrepreneurial." As testified by the afore-mentioned quote, for some learners, the challenge was how to do things for themselves having come from an educational system that had fed students through the teacher-led system. Table 6.1 presents a summary of the differences between traditional teacher-led approaches to EE as shown by Case 1 and the experiential TA model of EE as shown by Case 3. Case 2 presents a blended model. The differences range from the aims, role of instructors, intentions of students, and role of learners in teaching and learning.

Table 6.1 The role of teachers and learners in teacher-led entrepreneurship education compared with the Team Academy approach

Dimensions	Case 1	Case 2	Case 3
Course aims	• To provide knowledge and create awareness of entrepreneurship	• To train leaners to become entrepreneurial and entrepreneurs	• To train learners to become entrepreneurs and/or entrepreneurial
Teaching and learning approach	• Teacher led	• Teacher led with elements of experiential learning	• Experiential learning
Motivations of learners	• To acquire a degree • To acquire knowledge on entrepreneurship	• To acquire a degree • To acquire knowledge and become entrepreneurial and/or an entrepreneur	• To acquire a degree • To become an entrepreneur and/or entrepreneurial through real-world experiences and "learning-by-doing"

(*Continued*)

Table 6.1 (Continued)

Dimensions	Case 1	Case 2	Case 3
Learner's role	• Passive learning • Mostly individual learning • No reflection and self-awareness • Limited application of learning • Limited engagement with entrepreneurs • No engagement with customers • Limited application of learning	• Passive and active learning • Individual and limited team learning • Limited reflection and self-awareness • Limited engagement with entrepreneurs and business community • Application of learning	• Active learning • Team learning • Experiential and action learning • Reflection and self-awareness • Engagement with entrepreneurs and business community • Engagement with customers • Application of learning

Source: Authors' own.

EEL Framework

Recently, there have been calls for the implementation of experiential learning in entrepreneurship in higher education (see Hytti & O'Gorman, 2004; Matlay & Mitchell, 2006; European Commission, 2011, p. 10). The traditional teacher-led model of EE inspired by Bloom's (1956) taxonomy as shown by Case 1 enables learners to acquire conceptual knowledge and awareness about entrepreneurship. Yet, learners may soon forget what was learned as the approach does not encourage student's engagement, active learning, and the acquisition of important entrepreneurial competencies due to lack of concrete entrepreneurial experiences (Pittaway & Cope, 2007; Nabi et al., 2017).

To provide concrete entrepreneurial experiences to learners, a TA model illustrated by Case 3 draws on Kolb's (1984) ELT to implement experiential EE in higher education. Yet, there are challenges when implementing principles of experiential learning using Kolb's ELT model in higher education classrooms. According to Kolb's ELT model, the first phase of experiential learning requires learners to have concrete experiences which are later reflected on. With learners on undergraduate entrepreneurship courses in higher education not likely to have significant entrepreneurship experiences upon which to reflect, Kolb's first phase in experiential learning has limitations as learners cannot advance to the second stage of reflection without experiences. Furthermore, Kolb's ELT model may not equip learners with the concepts and theoretical knowledge that are needed to enable them to successfully deal with the complex issues in entrepreneurial learning (see Gibb, 2002). Attempts to address these challenges by implementing elements of Kolb's experiential learning in the traditional teacher-led classroom model of EE as shown by Case 2 also have limitations due to the lack of motivation of some learners on the traditional classroom teacher-led degree courses to engage in experiential learning. Drawing on these findings, we propose the EEL model (Figure 6.1) as a solution to the conundrum of EEL in higher education. The model marries elements of Bloom's (1956) traditional classroom and Kolb's (1984) experiential learning models in EE. Instructors can use EEL's phases of intention, concepts, experience, reflection, and experimentation to implement effective entrepreneurial experiential education in higher education.

EEL considers learner's motivations to engage in EEL to enable them to become active participants, autonomous, and creative learners who invest energy and efforts and thereby take responsibility for their learning through

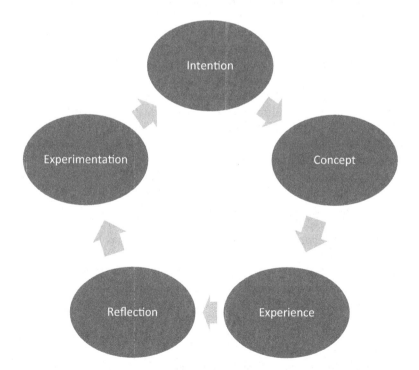

Figure 6.1 Entrepreneurial experiential learning model.

Source: Authors' own.

collaborations with the instructor and peers in order to achieve the desired personal development (Astin, 1984; Gibb, 2002). It also considers the need for learners to acquire significant conceptual and theoretical knowledge while engaging in hands-on experiences, reflection, and experimentation.

Intention: Intentions are the best predictors of planned behaviour (Azjen, 1991), and entrepreneurial intentions predict entrepreneurial action (Elfving et al., 2017; Krueger Jr et al., 2000). Hence, prior to starting the course, the learner needs to have the intention for entrepreneurial personal development through experiential learning. However, the intentions should be informed through the marketing information from the higher education institutions and interviews prior to admissions. This phase is not included in Kolb's ELT and hence was missing in Case 3.

Concept: Concept is when learners are confronted with key concepts and theories of entrepreneurship and are expected to understand and be able to utilise some of the concepts and ideas contained in them. This stage is similar to Bloom's knowledge and comprehension stages where learners are expected to remember ideas and materials (Bloom, 1956, pp. 62, 89). Concepts and knowledge are critically relevant to the achievement of positive results for the venture (Gibb, 2002), but that phase is missing from Kolb's ELT and the TA experiential entrepreneurship learning journey as shown by Case 3 in this study.

Experience: Concrete hands on experience of entrepreneurship through, for example, team building, ideation, market research, product development, finance, sales, and marketing, are important to educate the entrepreneur. These experiences initiate the learning process in practice but involve the application of the concepts already learned at the concept phase and in real-life experience. Hence, it is similar to Kolb's (1984) experience phase in terms of hands-on practical learning. However, unlike in Kolb's ELT model, it occurs after the concept phase as at the beginning of the undergraduate course, the learner's prior entrepreneurship experience may be very limited. Nonetheless, it is similar to Bloom's (1956) stage of application where the learner applies what has been learned in theory without being directed.

Reflection: Reflection on the experience and the concepts enable the learner to use critical thinking to reflect and explore other possibilities. This stage is similar to Kolb's (1984) phase of reflection and Bloom's stages of analysis and synthesis (Bloom, 1956). This phase enables the learner to breakdown the experiences and concepts to identify how the constituent parts relate to the whole.

Experimentation: The newly constructed theories borne out of the reflection are employed to make decisions after evaluation based on the concepts learned and the entrepreneurship experiences to ascertain if they were effective in practice or not. This stage is similar to Bloom's (1956) stage of evaluation and Kolb's (1984) stage of experiment. After experimentation, the learner intentionally initiates the next phase of learning based on the level of the course. Hence, the framework presents a cycle of learning.

In conclusion, this chapter draws on Bloom's (1956) and Kolb's (1984) models of learning and three cases to compare traditional teacher-led approach with TA experiential learning in entrepreneurship in higher education. The findings show that there are stark differences between traditional teacher-led models and experiential TA models of EE. In spite of the calls from scholars and policy makers to implement experiential learning (e.g. Fayolle & Toutain, 2013; QAA, 2018), this study shows that the use of either Bloom's (1956) taxonomy or Kolb's (1984) ELT model presents challenges in implementing experiential learning in entrepreneurship in higher education. Given these challenges, the EEL model provides a blended tool that marries some phases of Bloom's (1956) taxonomy used in the classroom and Kolb's (1984) ELT used in experiential learning. The entrepreneurship educator can utilize the phases of intention, concepts, experience, reflection, and experimentation to implement experiential learning in higher education while being sensitive to the need to include conceptualization and experience required by higher education.

Suggestions for Future Research

This study was based on three cases, and so future research can focus on testing the model using a larger sample of cases and/or a survey to validate the model. Entrepreneurship education has potential to enhance transformational entrepreneurship, which describes major changes in society influenced by entrepreneurial activity that enable enhanced socio-economic development. Further research is therefore required to explore educational practices that can support the development of transformational entrepreneurs (Maas & Jones, 2019).

References

Amoako, I. O. (2019). *Trust, institutions, and managing entrepreneurial organisations*. Palgrave. doi:10.1007/978-3-319-98395-0

Astin, A. W. (1984). Student involvement: A developmental theory for higher education. *Journal of College Student Personnel*, *25*(4), 297–308.

Azjen, I. (1991). The theory of planned behavior. *Organizational Behavior and Human Decision Processes*, *50*(2), 179–211.

Bloom, B. S. (1956). *Taxonomy of educational objectives: Vol. 1. Cognitive domain*. McKay, pp. 20, 24.

Braun, V., & Clarke, V. (2006). Using thematic analysis in psychology. *Qualitative Research in Psychology, 3*(2), 77–101. doi:10.1191/1478088706qp063oa

Chell, E. (2007). Social enterprise and entrepreneurship: Towards a convergent theory of the entrepreneurial process. *International Small Business Journal, 25*(1), 5–26. doi.org/10.1177/0266242607071779

Elfving, J., Brännback, M., & Carsrud, A. (2017). Revisiting a contextual model of entrepreneurial intentions. In *Revisiting the entrepreneurial mind* (pp. 83–90). Springer. doi:10.1007/978-3-319-45544-0_7

European Commission. (2008). *Entrepreneurship in higher education, especially within non-business studies.* Final Report of the Expert Group. Brussels: The Commission.

European Commission. (2011). *Entrepreneurship education: Enabling teachers as a critical success factor.* A report on teacher education and training to prepare teachers for the challenge of entrepreneurship education. Brussels: European Commission.

Fayolle, A., & Toutain, O. (2013). Four educational principles to rethink ethically entrepreneurship education. *Revista de economía mundial, 35,* 165–176.

Gibb, A. A. (1987). Enterprise culture – Its meaning and implications for education and training. *Journal of European Industrial Training, 11*(2), 2–38.

Gibbs, P. (2002). From the invisible hand to the invisible handshake: Marketing higher education. *Research in Post-Compulsory Education, 7*(3), 325–338. doi:10.1080/13596740200200134

Hytti, U., & O'Gorman, C. (2004). What is "enterprise education"? An analysis of the objectives and methods of enterprise education programmes in four European countries. *Education Training, 48*(1), 11–23. doi:10.1108/00400910410518188

Jones, B., & Iredale, N. (2006). Developing an entrepreneurial life skills summer school. *Innovations in Education and Teaching International, 43*(3), 233–244. doi:10.1080/14703290600618522

Jones, P., Mass, G., Kraus, S. and Lloyd Reason, L. (2021). Exploration of the role and contribution of entrepreneurship centres in UK higher education institutions. *Journal of Small Business and Entrepreneurship Development, 28*(2), 205–228.

Katz, J. A. (2003). The chronology and intellectual trajectory of American entrepreneurship education: 1876–1999. *Journal of Business Venturing, 18*(2), 283–300. doi:10.1016/S0883–9026(02)00098–8

Koellinger, P. D., & Roy Thurik, A. (2012). Entrepreneurship and the business cycle. *Review of Economics and Statistics, 94*(4), 1143–1156. doi:10.1162/REST_a_0022410.1162

Kolb, D. A. (1984). *Experiential learning: Experience as the source of learning and development.* Prentice-Hall.

Krueger Jr, N. F., Reilly, M. D., & Carsrud, A. L. (2000). Competing models of entrepreneurial intentions. *Journal of Business Venturing, 15*(5–6), 411–432. doi:10.1016/S0883–9026(02)00098–8

Lumpkin, G., & Bacq, S. (2019). Civic wealth creation: A new view of stakeholder engagement and societal impact. *Academy of Management Perspectives, 33*(4), 383–404. doi:10.5465/amp.2017.0060

Maas, G., & Jones, P. (2019). *Transformational entrepreneurship practices – Global case studies*. Palgrave. doi:10.1007/978-3-030-11524-1

Malmström, M., Johansson, J., & Wincent, J. (2017). Gender stereotypes and venture support decisions: How governmental venture capitalists socially construct entrepreneurs' potential. *Entrepreneurship Theory and Practice, 41*(5), 833–860. doi:10.1111/etap.12275

Matlay, H., & Mitchell, B. (2006). Entrepreneurship education in South Africa: A nationwide survey. *Education Training, 48*(5), 348–359. doi:10.1108/0040 0910610677054/

Minichiello, V., Aroni, R., & Hays, T. N. (2008). *In-depth interviewing: Principles, techniques, analysis*. Pearson Education, Australia.

Nabi, G., Liñán, F., Fayolle, A., Krueger, N., & Walmsley, A. (2017). The impact of entrepreneurship education in higher education: A systematic review and research agenda. *Academy of Management Learning & Education, 16*(2), 277–299.

Parker-Jenkins, M. (2018). Problematising ethnography and case study: Reflections on using ethnographic techniques and researcher positioning. *Ethnography and Education, 13*(1), 18–33. doi:10.1080/17457823.2016.1253028

Pittaway, L., & Cope, J. (2007). Entrepreneurship education: A systematic review of the evidence. *International Small Business Journal, 25*(5), 479–510. doi:10.1177/0266242607080656

Pittaway, L., & Edwards, C. (2012). Assessment: Examining practice in entrepreneurship education. *Education and Training, 54*(8), 778-800.

Preedy, S., Jones, P., Maas, G., & Duckett, H. (2020). Examining the perceived value of extracurricular enterprise activities in relation to entrepreneurial learning processes. *Journal of Small Business and Enterprise Development, 27*(7). doi:10.1108/JSBED-12-2019-0408

QAA. (2018). *Enterprise and entrepreneurship: Guidance for UK higher education providers*. Retrieved on September 12, 2020, from www.qaa.ac.uk/en/Publications/Documents/Enterprise-and-entrpreneurship-education-2018.pdf

Shane, S. (2000). Prior knowledge and the discovery of entrepreneurial opportunities. *Organization Science, 11*(4), 448–469. doi:10.1287/orsc.11.4.448.14602

Shane, S., & Venkataraman, S. (2000). The promise of entrepreneurship as a field of research. *Academy of Management Review, 25*(1), 217–226. doi:10.5465/amr.2000.27

7 Team Coaching

A Review (on Where We Are Now) and Recommendations for Moving Forward the Practice

Uwe Napiersky

The History, Concept, and Definition of Team Coaching

Team coaching[1] is a relatively new but growing concept within the business world (Carr & Peters, 2012) and frequently is regarded as an extension of individual coaching. The notion of coaching itself is still quite new too. Coaching appeared in the 1970s and grew exponentially at the end of the 20th century or at the beginning of the 21st century (Hawkins, 2014). As an illustration, the ICF (International Coaching Federation) was created only 22 years ago, and in their 2016 Global Coaching Study, the ICF does not even mention team coaching. According to Hawkins (2014, p. 63), team coaching is "currently 20 years behind" compared to the evidence-based research in 1:1 coaching, which highlights the academic messiness in TC, especially in providing evidence of its effectiveness or definition of the concept. Team coaching, compared to 1 to 1 coaching, can be seen as more complex due to a different set of dynamics, as it will be explained later.

Inspired by a map of coaching origins from the researcher and practitioner de Haan some years ago, with colleagues and MSc students, I did an initial literature research which revealed that origins of TC echo a hybrid discipline, emerging from different disciplines, approaches, and theories, as shown in Figure 7.1.

The submarines and ladders shown in Figure 7.1 illustrate the continuous cross fertilization from fields like sport coaching, psychology, team theories, leadership theories, and one-to-one coaching. As an example of evidence-based research in the TC field, you find Wotruba (2016) on the right side of the illustration on the island of team coaching. Her research is about the importance of trust in the TC process and represented more recent evidence-based research in the year 2017, when we created this map of origins of TC. In the middle of the team coaching island (on the right side of the map), there are Hackman and Wageman, (2005) and Clutterbuck (2007),

DOI: 10.4324/9781003163091-8

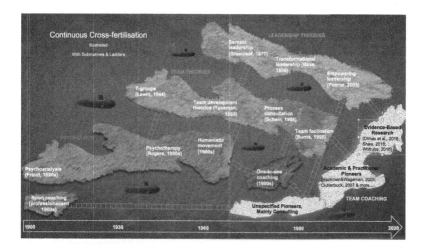

Figure 7.1 A map of team coaching origins.

Source: Napiersky, Chretien, & Jones (2017, internal, not published paper).

who are academic pioneers in the field, and there are lots of unspecified pioneers on this team coaching island, mainly consultancies and coaching and team experienced practitioners who lend a hand in an early stage on this new team intervention concept.

Not surprisingly there were lots of TC practice and practitioner-oriented literature; however, it motivated two colleagues and me to research the distinctiveness of TC because there was and maybe still is a lot of confusion and messiness about what TC exactly is.

Regarding academic models of TC, like the aforementioned Hackman and Wageman's (2005) theory of TC, we saw it as not sufficient for capturing the range of TC scenarios that occur in practice. Further, the model is still to be empirically tested or validated. In the absence of any alternative models or frameworks on TC per se, the field of TC can consequently be termed as a pre-theory stage (p. 64),[2] and in accordance with Hastings and Pennington (2019), I see it as crucial that testable theoretical TC frameworks should be developed that can guide the research into TC effectiveness. The absence of clarity on the definition and conceptualization of TC is problematic for both theory development and empirical exploration (Kohler et al., 2017) if it wants to be applied in a learning and education research setting with verifiable quality control mechanisms.

Such analyses and conceptualization are important as well for organizations or institutions to understand what exactly they are buying and why.

In a global study in which 410 team coaches took part and which also contained a systematic literature analysis, we made an attempt to close the gap of an evidence-based definition.[3]

In a first step in our study, we reviewed 15 TC definitions, which were obtained from peer-reviewed and ranked academic journals, in order to see what was accomplished so far and to explore the notion of TC. An overview of all these definition about TC from 2001 to 2018 are listed in our research paper,[4] Figure 7.2 shows identified keywords, sorted into a hierarchical structure.

The range of content in the explored definitions of TC also revealed a substantial overlap between many elements of the TC definitions and the definitions of team training, team building, and team development, which we analysed via a literature review too.

Brief Excursion: Team Training, Team Building, and Team Development

- *Team training* is seen as a key and systematic strategy to improve team effectiveness and aims at knowledge, skills, and/or attitudes of teamwork in order to improve performance.
- *Team building* is a process intervention that prompts team members to reflect on their behaviour and interpersonal relationships. Team building consists of four elements: goal setting, interpersonal relationships, clarification of roles, and problem solving.
- *Team development* is an informal, holistic process that team members go through together, whereby the members try to create effective social structures and work processes for themselves. In general, it can be stated that the studies on targeted interventions for learning and developing teams focus on one main differentiating factor, namely, whether it is about special tasks or team processes.

In Table 7.1, we summarize the key themes from the TC definitions and illustrate the overlap with other team learning and development interventions.

Key subjects in the explored existing TC literature specified that TC involves:

- problem solving,
- raising awareness or use of reflection,
- a focus on teamwork,
- process,
- goals and objectives with a systematic approach.

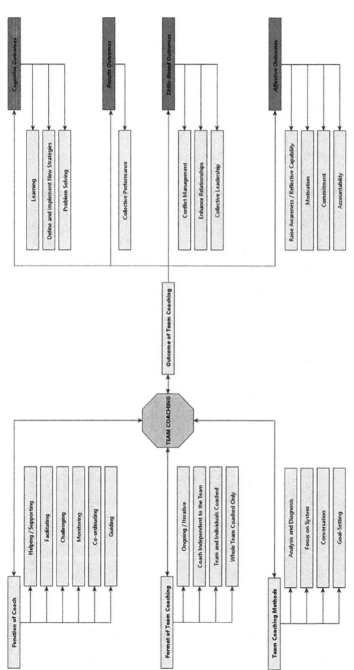

Figure 7.2 Hierarchical structure of themes from the team coaching definition literature.

Source: Jones et al. (2019).

Table 7.1 Comparison of team coaching themes with definitions of team training, building, and development + team coaching

Themes	Description	Team-interventions	Team coaching definitions
1. Common team goal	Team coaching is focused on achieving a common or shared goal.	X, TT, TB	X
2. Focus on team performance	The desired output or outcome of team coaching improved team performance.	X, TT, TB	X
3. Team learning and reflection	Team coaching achieves team learning via self and team member reflections.	X, TB, TD	X
4. Team coaching activities	The methodology, actions, or processes whereby a team coach enables improvement in the teams' capability to achieve their shared goal and improve team performance. Includes raising awareness, improving communication, and building trusting relationships.	X, TB, TD	X
5. Team as a system	A team is formed of an interconnecting network of individuals. This complex whole is the focus of the team coaching (rather than the individuals within it).	X, TD	X
6. Advanced coaching skills	Team coaching required advanced coaching skills due to the complexity of coaching a group of individuals at the same time. Includes simultaneously understanding multiple perspectives; observe and interpret interactions; understanding of team facilitation techniques; and psychological safety, i.e., ability to build trust to enable effective openness and sharing between team members.		
7. Coaching techniques	Application of coaching techniques to achieve team goals and improve team performance. Includes effective questioning and abstaining from providing guidance or instruction.		Partly
8. Long term	Team coaching is usually provided over a relatively long term.		

X= yes, is in current team coaching definitions; TT = team training; TB = team building; TD = team development

Source: Based on Jones et al. (2019).

All the aforementioned elements are also present in the definitions of at least one or sometimes more of the other forms of team learning and development interventions.[5] When viewing the range of TC definitions in the context of other team learning and development definitions, it was clear that TC is yet to be concisely defined in a way that based on Donaldson et al. (2013) provides sufficient clarity, rigour, and distinctiveness for organizational management theory research. Without this clear conceptualization of TC, it is impossible to progress research onto more pertinent questions such as how and why TC works, or even if it works at all (Shepherd & Suddaby, 2017).

Also, it was interesting to see the variations in the team coaching definitions, and we understood why the academic TC arena was described as messy. The general themes of the function or role of the coach, the outcomes from TC, the TC methods, and the format of TC can be identified across many of the definitions; nevertheless, there was little agreement at the next level. For example, the role of the team coach was conceptualized in six different ways across the 15 definitions. The definitions also included contradictions such as coaching the team as a whole vs coaching individual team members or no specification regarding either.

On the basis of 410 web-based interviews and our analysis, we[6] recommended the following evidence-based definition of TC:

- Team coaching is a team-based learning and development intervention that considers the team to be a system and is applied collectively to the team as a whole.
- The focus of team coaching is on team performance and the achievement of a common or shared team goal.
- Team learning is empowered via specific team coaching activities for self-reflection and team reflection, which are facilitated by the team coach(es) through the application of coaching techniques such as impactful, reflective questioning which raises awareness, builds trusting relationships, and improves communication.
- A team coach does not provide advice or solutions to the team. Rather, team coaching requires advanced coaching skills from the coach such as considering multiple perspectives simultaneously and observing and interpreting dynamic interactions and is typically provided over a series of sessions rather than as a one-off intervention.

Our evidence-based definition of TC can also be differentiated from definitions of one-to-one coaching. The TC definition implies to the team level and unambiguously captures the distinct dynamic nature of TC, as well as the characteristic complexities of managing individual perspectives and intra-team dynamics in the coaching process at the same time. Furthermore, in our definition, the vehicle for change is collective learning, with the desired outcome being team (rather than individual) performance.

TC Competencies

In order to create a set of TC competencies, the ICF designed and conducted an evidence-based research project at the end of 2019.[7] the ICF, a one of the biggest coaching associations globally, obviously recognized the emerging field of TC and the importance to support guidance for the professionalising of TC. The aim of this study was to establish which knowledge, skills, abilities, and other qualities (KSAO) that team coaches apply in addition to the ICF core competencies (referring to the one-to-one coaching competencies). The following activities were undertaken: A comprehensive literature review, development of team coaching critical incidents, task, and KSAO virtual workshops to garner an understanding of the experience of team coaching and how it differs from one-to-one coaching and semi-structured interviews to understand how team coaches experience coaching engagements and what team coaching means to them as a profession, a global survey to determine the importance of specific team coaching tasks and KAOs and their relationship to facilitation, and competency model workshops to review all of the job analysis data.[8]

It is a delight to see that this rigorous research project provides some clarity about TC competencies. See the TC from the ICF in Table 7.2.

Table 7.2 ICF team coaching competencies 2020

	Competency	Definition
1	Demonstrates ethical practice	Understands and consistently applies coaching ethics and standards of coaching.
2	Embodies a coaching mindset	Develops and maintains a mindset that is open, curious, flexible, and client centred.
3	Establishes and maintains agreements	Partners with the client and relevant stakeholders to create clear agreements about the coaching relationship, process, plans, and goals. Establishes agreements for the overall coaching engagement as well as those for each coaching session.
4	Cultivates trust and safety	Partners with the client to create a safe, supportive environment that allows the client to share freely. Maintains a relationship of mutual respect and trust.
5	Maintains presence	Is fully conscious and present with the client, employing a style that is open, flexible, grounded, and confident.

(*Continued*)

Table 7.2 (Continued)

Competency	Definition
6 Listens actively	Focuses on what the client is and is not saying to fully understand what is being communicated in the context of the client systems and to support client self-expression.
7 Evokes awareness	Facilitates client insight and learning by using tools and techniques such as powerful questioning, silence, metaphor, or analogy.
8 Facilitates client growth	Partners with the client to transform learning and insight into action. Promotes client autonomy in the coaching process.

Source: Author's own.

The ICF notes as well that further research is necessary. They refer to caution when considering integrating team coaching with team training, consulting, or mentoring, which hints to the brief excursion earlier in this chapter about team training, development, and building. Furthermore, a crisp distinction between team coaching and facilitation may not be there. Reading the ICF TC research report, the multi-faceted nature of TC becomes apparent, and further evidence-based research is obviously needed. Nevertheless, this TC competencies insight is an important milestone for the TC theory development, guidance for practitioners, and designer for TC education.

It is helpful as well as the recommendation of supervision for team coaches due to the complexity of the work and ease with which a team coach can get caught up in internal team dynamics.

Reflections on the Tiimiakatemia Model of Team Coaching and Other TC Approaches

In the context of this book, I want to share some observations and reflections on the *Tiimiakatemia* (TA) model of team coaching. Blackwood et al. (2015) share in their conference paper observations and perceptions gained from conversations and discussions, interviews, focus groups, and team meetings about the entrepreneurial business management (EBM) course of TA in a university in the United Kingdom. They claim that team coaching replaces traditional lectures and classroom teaching to support a flexible learning approach. Each team is assigned a coach who is responsible for creating an environment conducive to promoting effective learning and personal development within the team (Blackwood et al., 2015). Tiimiakatemia Global (2016) shares the mystical principles of the team coach as leading thoughts, which echoes the innovation drive of this approach and their team coaches. These are valuable forerunner thoughts and worthy of underpinning with real evidence, to bring it out of the *mystery* space. Fowle and Jussila (2016, p. 1) state that Team Coaching sessions are critical to the success of the EBM programme. In addition, they report:

> The international Team Academy network is a major source of support in the sharing of best practice and generation of new ideas. There will always be a tension in the UK between the drive to create and apply innovative teaching methods and the formal obligation to collect evidence to justify academic awards to programme participants.

In general, I agree with the final statement of Fowle & Jussila (p. 10) that the "TA story is just the beginning." The TA model itself has a lot of potential to provide an entrepreneurial and innovation mindset for the learner. Compared to our evidence-based definition of TC, the TA model emphasises collective team learning. There might also be a lot of overlap between TA team coaches' competencies and the above ICF TC competencies. Evidence-based research might help to bring more insight and clarity about that.

Widdowson et al. (2020) point out that TC itself can benefit from approaches and insights from different disciplines. Also in their TC literature review, they mention insights from the fields of coaching, team coaching, group coaching, family therapy, group dynamics, gestalt, team development, team effectiveness, systems thinking, transactional analysis, constellations, reflective practice, and supervision. The TA model should be included in this list of approaches to benefit the TC arena.

Final Conclusions

As popular as it has become, TC is still an emerging discipline, and it is debatable whether it is still in a pre-theory stage. As mentioned earlier, the field is filled with contradictions but lots of potential. However, despite the many questions about how precisely TC works, how to measure TC success, and so on, TC appears to be one of the most valuable, adaptable, and efficient new leadership/learner/student development tools available. In fact, its adaptability and resourcefulness probably make clear in some part why it is so difficult to quantify and define it. From a wider point of view, it would be advantageous to compare TC with other team skill building, team behaviour change, and team leadership/learner/student development interventions. Yet the comparability to other team interventions makes it cumbersome.

Even so, if team coaches continue to seek better ways to help teams (of leaders/learners/students) accelerate their learning, improve performance, and well-being, TC itself is likely to continue to flourish long into the future.

Notes

1. Just to clarify: The terms and notion of 'group coaching' and 'team coaching' are different and to use them interchangeably is misleading, (Brown & Grant, 2010). Team coaching is different from group coaching because of the emphasis on capacity building of a team, team effectiveness, team values and shared behavioural norms (Britton, 2015).
2. Jones, R. J., Napiersky, U., & Lyubovnikova, J. (2019). Conceptualizing the distinctiveness of team coaching. *Journal of Managerial Psychology, 34*(2),
3. Jones, R. J., Napiersky, U., & Lyubovnikova, J. (2019). Conceptualizing the distinctiveness of team coaching. *Journal of Managerial Psychology, 34*(2).
4. As footnote 3.
5. As footnote 3.
6. As footnote 3.
7. Personally, I had the honour to be involved in this team coaching competency job analysis as a subject matter expert (SME) among 20 plus global SMEs.
8. See: https://coachingfederation.org/app/uploads/2020/11/Team-Coaching-Com petencies-2.pdf

References

Blackwood, T., Baty, G., Dale, B., Fowle, M., Hatt, L., Jussila, N., & Pugalis, L. (2015). *Team Academy Northumbria – Learn to surprise yourself.* [Online], The Higher Education Academy, Compendium of Effective Practice in Directed Independent Learning. Retrieved on June 2020, from, www.academia.edu/download/41120898/Team_Academy_Northumbria__learn_to_surprise_yourself_HEA_Accepted_Peer_Reviewed_Final_Version_Sep_2014.pdf

Britton, J. (2015). *From one to many: Best practices for team and group coaching.* Jossey-Bass, Toronto, Canada.

Brown, S. W., & Grant, A. M. (2010). From grow to group: Theoretical issues and a practical model for group coaching in organisations. *Coaching: An International Journal of Theory, Research and Practice, 3*(1), 30–45. doi:10.1080/17521880903559697

Carr, C., & Peters, J. (2012). *The experience and impact of team coaching: A dual case study* (Ph.D., Middlesex University).

Clutterbuck, D. (2007). *Coaching the team at work.* Nicholas Brealey Publishing.

Donaldson, L., Qiu, J., & Luo, B. N. (2013). For rigour in organizational management theory research. *Journal of Management Studies, 50*(1), 153–172.

Fowle, M., & Jussila, N. (2016, September). The adoption of a Finnish Learning Model in the UK. In *European Conference on Innovation and Entrepreneurship* (p. 194). Academic Conferences International Limited.

Hackman, J., & Wageman, R. (2005). A theory of team coaching. *Academy of Management Review*, [online], *30*(2), 269–287. www.jstor.org/stable/20159119

Hastings, R., & Pennington, W. (2019). Team coaching: A thematic analysis of methods used by external coaches in a work domain. *International Journal of Evidence Based Coaching and Mentoring, 17*(2), 174–188. doi:10.24384/akra-6r08

Hawkins, P. (Ed.). (2014). *Leadership team coaching in practice: Developing high-performing teams*. Kogan Page Publishers.

Jones, R. J., Napiersky, U., & Lyubovnikova, J. (2019). Conceptualizing the distinctiveness of team coaching. *Journal of Managerial Psychology*, *34*(2), 62–78. doi:10.1108/JMP-07-2018-0326

Kohler, T., Landis, R. S., & Cortina, J. M. (2017). Establishing methodological rigor in quantitative management learning and education research: The role of design, statistical methods, and reporting standards. *Academy of Management Learning & Education*, *16*(2), 173–192. doi:10.5465/amle.2017.0079

Mann, C. (2015). *The 6th Ridler report: Strategic trends in the use of executive coaching*. Retrieved on January 26, 2020, from www.associationforcoaching.com/media/uploads/6th_ridler_report_-_joint_icf,_ac_and_emcc_webinar,_december_2015_-_presentation_slides.pdf

Shepherd, D. A., & Suddaby, R. (2017). Theory building: A review and integration. *Journal of Management*, *43*(1), 59–86.

Tiimiakatemia Global. (2016). *Leading thoughts*. [Online]. Retrieved on January 2, 2021, from http://tiimiakatemia.com/en/company/leading-thoughts

Widdowson, L., Rochester, L., Barbour, P. J., & Hullinger, A. M. (2020). Bridging the team coaching competency gap: A review of the literature. *International Journal of Evidence Based Coaching & Mentoring*, *18*(2).

Wotruba, S. (2016). Leadership Team Coaching: A trust-based coaching relationship. *International Journal of Evidence Based Coaching and Mentoring*, [online], *10*, 98–109. http://ijebcm.brookes.ac.uk

8 Why Team Academy?

Chris Jackson

Taking any new product to market can be a struggle, especially if it's innovative, perceived to be "ahead of its time" or it challenges the status quo. Getting people to change or adapt their behaviour, without them being able to fully identify an immediately apparent reason, need, or benefit, can be met with resistance and scepticism. *Why do we need this? What we have already works fine.*

And so it is with the Team Academy (TA) model. Why should we give up on an ages-old pedagogical model of teaching which is embraced worldwide? A model of the *sage on the stage* where the teacher is the expert; the curriculum is decided, controlled, and measured; and success of institution and pupil are based on pre-defined proximal outputs. The world of work is little different, and organisations, large and small, look for training, advisors, and consultants to provide solutions to growth requirements or answers to *problems*.

But what if we are being myopic and ignoring the inevitable? What if we are part of a social evolutionary process that demands that change in the way we are *taught* is not only unavoidable but necessary? What if traditional models of teaching can no longer keep up with our need to learn? Emerging literature and commentary would suggest that team learning is not just a *new thing* but an inescapable and necessary response to a world where uncertainty, change, and complexity demand reactions where an *expert* prescribing a single or universally accepted solution becomes a nonsense. One-size answers certainly do not fit all clients.

So what is the point of TA? Is it just an interesting and innovative educational model that will amuse minds and provide research activities for academics until another *flavour of the month* emerges, or is it something far broader than this? Is it indeed part of an evolutionary, learning necessity – a phenomenon whose time has now come?

What might a global TA network look like? What would be its purpose? Why should we promote it? Is this a black art that is to remain in the domain of academia? Is it a virus that has already been released?

DOI: 10.4324/9781003163091-9

Or could it be an antidote to a much deeper, embedded problem in that the way that we teach is not wholly appropriate for tomorrow's world?

In order to make sense of this, I'd like to share some of my own personal learning journey with you. It is a journey of the reflexive praxis of an entrepreneur, not a commentary or analysis by a bystander. In saying this, I also need to be clear about my personal belief with regard to the term *entrepreneur*:

I believe that*: an entrepreneur is an individual who has a capacity to interpret their task environment in ways in which they may subsequently add value to situations which may be problematic or for which there are few perceived resolutions. In doing this they will not only develop their own "world-view" (G. weltanschauung) but possibly – and certainly within established organisations – alienate others by taking what are otherwise deemed to be unacceptable risks that may not subscribe to accepted causal management practices.*

A person who starts a business venture is not necessarily an entrepreneur – and if they are, this is far from a guarantee of success as measured by business support and government organisations. Until convinced otherwise, I believe that some people are born with the traits and attributes that allow them to naturally be entrepreneurial; to others, this can be encouraged or mimicked to some extent; for some it is an alien and uncomfortable state.

I also make no apology for the style in which I'm offering this story and my thoughts to you. This is not meant to be an academic treatise – it's written to offer the reader both insight and foresight to a world – my world – of entrepreneurial learning, how this might occur and why it might be even more appropriate across society in general.

When I was at senior school, the careers advice that we were offered was pretty shoddy. Mine was in the form of, Ah, but you'll stay on and take your A-levels and then go to university!

It was at this point that I learned what has turned out to be one of the most powerful questions in a coach's armoury:

Why . . . .?

Subsequently stolen by Simon Sinek, I realized pretty early on that this must be a neat question, as it is frequently met with silence, confusion, or anger. Sometimes, it is met with all three of these responses (not necessarily in that order) so I advocate use with caution. Both my career advisor (who was also the PE teacher) and my parents seemed to have some difficulty with the question, although my parents (both teachers) in their wisdom, and came up with a working fix. Or perhaps it was an ultimatum:

> If you can find yourself a job that offers training, then you can leave school without taking A-levels. If you can't find a job by the end of term, then you will stay on and take your A-levels. . .

In doing this, I don't think that they realized the amazing start they were offering me to my working life. *More school* was exactly what I didn't want at this stage. More school, then even more school – even if it was in the shape of a university – sounded like a life sentence. I had no idea what I wanted to do, but what I did know was that it was time for me to get out and DO something.

I rose to my parents' challenge, identified *jobs with training*, and ended up being accepted for an apprenticeship by a major national corporation. I started *work* two weeks after leaving school aged 16, only to discover that six weeks later, they were sending me back to another version of *school* – a further education college. Which is where something unusual happened.

For years, I had struggled with mathematics. Addies-ups and takies-away were fine, but trigonometry, algebra, and other dark arts just made no sense to me at all. I excelled at engineering drawing, having a natural ability to visualise things in more than one dimension. My English composition was OK, physics and chemistry acceptable, I loved geography, but maths? Why? It was almost as mysterious as Latin.

Bizarrely, after a few hiccups, maths now became my best subject. This was undoubtedly because I was now studying electrical engineering and on a daily basis I was working with volts, amps, ohms, and farads, all of which are explained with electrical theory which in turn is glued together with maths (and physics and some other stuff). Maths, at long last had a purpose. Maths in isolation, as a process or a theory without a means of application, was useless to me. It wasn't worth remembering.

That is, it was useless to me until I needed it.

So why, in most of the world, do we continue to teach to curricula determined by observers, normally at the expense of creativity, personal attributes and relevant application?

I didn't last for too long *doing* electrical engineering and I resigned from my first, perfectly sensible job-for-life at the tender age of 22, with nothing more than a desire to carve my own way in the world and a belief that I could. I did not have an ambition to be financially wealthy, but needed freedom, exploration and adventure. I was, and hopefully always will be, immensely curious – not good for cats as I understand, but essential if you have an appetite for the path less travelled by.

One of the things I had discovered as I began my apprenticeship was that there is a big, wide, fascinating, diverse world out there, where not many people are too impressed by your ability to regurgitate theory – they're more interested in what you can do, or perhaps more importantly, what you have done. I also discovered that I didn't get on very well working for people with little authenticity, or for organizations with little vision or a will to improve. It was time for some self-determined learning – *heutagogy* before it was given a name – and my career as *merchant adventurer* was launched.

This isn't an essay about entrepreneurship, but rather about what I would call entrepreneurial learning. In order not to wander too far off-plan, we now need to leap forward some 40 years so that I can offer you some provenance to what I am sharing. Needless to say, the intervening years were, let's say, formative. I am living proof that Nonaka and Takeuchi's Model of Knowledge Creation (1995) (probably) works – and the more you allow this to become an unconscious *subroutine (unconscious competence. . . .?)* the more you want to learn. It feeds the curious.

Distilling the full journey, the raw and potent sprit looks something like this:

- Became self-employed
- Incorporated first business
- Grew business
- Did lots of stuff
- Sold business
- Ran away to sea and started second business
- Decided that it was time for a change, stuck a pin in a map, and moved to a different part of the UK trading wild beaches and remote islands for rolling fields and trees.
- Collided with academia and began a new adventure

That's as much as we have time for here, but I'm sure you get the gist of life thus far. Perhaps we can dip back into the journey as I reflect on points as they're raised.

2020 saw me relocated in rural Lincolnshire, working as a Team Coach in the nascent business department of a small university delivering a business programme based on the Finnish Team Academy, or Tiimiakatemia, philosophy of team learning. This was not something that I had planned or thought of, and the result of some serendipitous meetings as I began to navigate my new and self-enforced task environment some five years earlier.

I've immersed myself in the practice and study (note the order – action first) of entrepreneurial team learning. I've completed a course of International Team Mastery; I've travelled throughout Europe and am both proud and humbled to be part of a now-global network of amazing people – fellow travellers who appreciate, promote and encourage the phenomenon that is entrepreneurship, through team learning.

So that's all good then? Job done?

No. Job starting. Because it would appear that for many, the TA way of learning isn't seen to be *academic enough*. It is viewed with scepticism. It is seen as *resource intensive*. It removes the *teacher as the expert*. Some even say it's cult-like. Yet – whatever *it* is – it would appear that *it* works.

Despite a laudable track record in Finland, where the programme had its genesis over 25 years ago, this does not offer enough efficacy for it to become an acceptable mainstream delivery model elsewhere. Academia requires theory and research in order to validate provenance. Change isn't necessarily good, it's scary. Change suggests *replacement*, which in turn could suggest that any previous state is no longer suitable or may indeed be flawed. In academia, seeing is not necessarily believing. Being *wrong* is not acceptable. Failure is scary and to be shunned.

I first *saw*, or experienced, TA at the University of the West of England (UWE), in the UK. I was invited to take part in a *learning expedition* – a short two-day visit to see what TA was all about.

What did I see? What did I learn?

I saw a group of young, enthusiastic, engaging people who were passionate about their course and the journey they were on. I had my first encounter with a *team coach*, who didn't seem to do very much; I had fun joining in with activities they had prepared for us. I saw something that, based on my life experience to-date, made immediate sense.

So what?

I didn't realise it at the time, but this was the beginning of a whole new journey for me too. Somewhere in the distillation process that I mentioned earlier, I did pass through a *filter* of academic learning that saw me emerge with a master's degree and expanded my ability to think. However, although I'd experienced life as a (mature) student, I had managed to escape the machinations of institutional academia. So, when I experienced TA for the first time, I had no other delivery process to compare it with – apart from my own learning journey as an entrepreneur.

Five years down the line, and I find myself as Programme Leader of a tiny cohort of students, constantly arguing as to why *my* programme should not be shelved in favour of *more traditional offers that guarantee bums on seats*. Yes, it rather looks as if I am *poacher turned gamekeeper*.

For me, I have spent a lifetime looking for ways to engage stakeholders in my business activities and have actively (and successfully) sold many things ranging from locks and safes to wildlife holidays. What have I learned from this? Difference sells. Discounting any academic argument, here is a product that's newsworthy. Here's a product with a USP.

However, they're still not currently interested.

So here, perhaps, is a tension – universities are run as academic institutions, not commercial organizations. In general, they are generally risk-averse and not keen to dabble with *new things*. Their prime driver is a need to constantly appease a galaxy of regulatory standards that require boxes to be ticked that will at least maintain their position in some national survey or other. They are also paranoid about student satisfaction surveys, work allocation modules, reports, results, recruitment figures. . . . If only they were as passionate about future-fit learning.

Or entrepreneurial learning.

As part of my Team Coach training, I have visited Finland several times now as the *alma mater*, the genesis, of TA – or Tiimiakatemia. Experiencing TA in action – without realising at the time what constraints different regimes or cultures might place on individual programmes – one of my first thoughts on experiencing TA was, *where else? Who else?* What I was experiencing was the condensation of the journey I had been on for many years, that *path less travelled by*, compressed into a degree course. Yet, however, amazing this new experience may appear to be, I can't help but feel that this *formalization* raises a caveat in that there is the potential to make entrepreneurial learning a little exclusive – what about those without, or who have missed out on, the opportunity of learning in this way?

Viral marketing is a term that appeared a little over 20 years ago in the heady days of the beginnings of the *online* revolution. It used to infer the rapid promotion of a product or service via social networks. Is it possible that TA is a form of as *viral learning*? Instead of people waiting around being told what to do by *experts*, what if there was a better understanding of the nature of *teams* (as in, they aren't just a collection of people who may need to do something) and *entrepreneurship* (as in, this is no longer simply about running a business for financial gain at the expense of others, but about combining resource to add value). What if this model could also be rolled out outside of the constraints of formal education allowing social communities to form entrepreneurial ecosystems or communities of practice that could determine for themselves what they needed to do and also knew how to go about filling in any gaps in their knowledge that was preventing them from doing this?

This might sound quite utopian, and I'm sure that trainers, advisors, consultants and (some) educators the world over would throw their hands up in horror at the thought of prospective students and clients suddenly working out for themselves what it is they need to be doing and how to do it. The old ways of command and control, expert and pupil, and have and have-not have worked for centuries, why on earth would we want to change anything?

I'd like to share three other reflections with you, one from my previous business existence and two from my current academic adventure:

1. As my first business grew, I realised that I could no longer do everything and that attempting to micromanage every process was not only unnecessary but unhealthy. I also knew that money wasn't the only motivator for those who worked with me – they genuinely wanted to be good at their jobs and take on more responsibility. We were early adopters of I.T. and (for both the size of the business and the era) had effective accounting and CRM systems in place. I offered some of the office staff the opportunity to attend our local college and work towards an accountancy qualification – even thought this would be in their own time, they jumped at the chance.

   The morning after they'd attended their class, we'd have a coffee together and I'd ask them what they'd covered the night before and let them explain how they *made sense* of this in their work environment. Any changes they wanted to make to our processes were encouraged. However, it didn't take them long to rumble their *trainer* at the college and discover that although they knew their way through whichever text book that needed to be followed, they fell flat on their face if asked a question that was *off plan*. The lecturer knew the mechanics – the theory – of the subject but had no experience of practical application. For my shining stars, their learning didn't happen until they brought it back to the workplace where it could be discussed and tested. At college, they learned very little of value *the sage on the stage* was a phoney.

2. The TA process is built around *learning by doing* – self-determined learning as individuals and in teams. It all sounds very exciting, but it can also be very scary for the learners. I have known students who have joined the course having gained top marks in business subjects at school and college become totally paralysed at the prospect of actually doing something. Taking action is scary. No one has told them how to do that. For some, this is simply too much, and they leave the course (*a good reason why this type of learning shouldn't be seen as an "easy ride" and probably warrants a careful selection process as seen in Finland and elsewhere in Europe*).

   I clearly remember one young lad – realising that he now had to DO something – approaching me like a frightened rabbit in headlights.

"What's up?" I asked as he stood in front of me wide-eyed and visibly shaken.

"I . . . I . . . don't know what to do . . . !", he spluttered.

"OK. Don't panic. What do you think you could do . . . ?"

At which point the spell was broken and he described the first steps he was going to take in building his new venture. We still laugh about this *unshackling* experience when we now meet.

One of the issues I persistently experience with young learners is that there is a *danger zone* between ideation and action that they are terrified to enter. They have never been equipped with the tools that they need to competently navigate the zone in which it becomes necessary to DO something – ANYTHING! Some even struggle when facing the challenge of coming up with any new ideas and seem to have inherent inability – almost a *learned helplessness* – to be curious and dare to find out what they don't yet know.

Their schooling today has let them down. They have sat in the lessons. They have passed the end of term quiz. They actually know very little.

3. I won't win many friends in academia with my next statement: I say to new students:

> You are here at university to gain a degree qualification. You can do that by playing the game of academia, in that, if you follow the rules, complete your assignments and answer the questions that you are asked in the acceptable format and therefor attain good marks, the University will award you a degree. But I want more than that for you. Some of you may go on to start your own businesses. Some of you will go on to work for other organisations. Either way – that's fine – but once you leave the safety of university, you're on your own and I don't care much for your chances if the only thing between you and the next person is a piece of paper. I need you to be different. I need you to be the ones who stand out.

And sometimes, this falls on stony ground, but for those who immerse themselves in what has become known in TA as *the process* there is not only a transformation but also often a transcendence. This is what I have witnessed working in a regime where *student attributes* are viewed as an *also ran* to core learning, being offered as an extra-curricular award.

And therefore, my challenge to any teacher, educator, trainer, mentor, or coach is this: in working with your student(s) what is it that you are learning together? Because if you're not, I'd suggest there's a danger that your thinking is not straying beyond what might be called *explicit* or proximal learning and that it may well not be future fit.

I have now told you my story, and it's time to conclude this chapter. I hope that in relating real-life experiences to you that you are able to relate to insights from a journey not yet complete. When my students are struggling with an assignment, I often say, *Let's go back to the question – what is it asking you to do?* So, let's just reconsider the point of this chapter:

Why Team Academy?

In order to offer an answer to this question, let's consider another*: What are we learning for and how are we doing this . . . ?*

In his foreword to the brilliant *Building Top Performing Teams* by Lucy Widdowson and Paul Barbour, Professor Peter Hawkins talks of the ability of organizations to become future fit. Surely it follows that, in order to be able to achieve this maxim, then our *learning* is also to be future fit.

Of course, we cannot accurately predict the future; therefore, we cannot predict precisely *what* it is we need to learn – but that is not the meaning of future fit. A more accurately statement may be that we need to adopt a future fit *way* of learning, embracing a paradigm shift in what is, in general, currently on offer as *teaching* and *training* and re-thinking *how* we learn. The world in which we all live, and *for* which we learn, is a VUCA (*volatile, uncertain, complex and ambiguous*) environment where *wicked problems* abound. It is no longer the domain of the Heroic Leader, and entrepreneurship no longer defines the profit-fuelled journey of the stellar business icon, but rather the realm of agile teams who can add value.

At which point I'd like to offer a final reflection on my time at sea. Learning to sail is a complex process, and competence is built by combining practice and theory. It's possibly the ultimate reflexive experience.

But there's not much than can prepare you for your first storm, other than an implicit belief in the integrity of your vessel and crew coupled with your own ability to use all of your senses to interpret myriad inputs of ever-changing information that assaults your senses. A planned course can become like a business plan in a pandemic – irrelevant – as you quickly respond to an emerging situation which could lead to discomfort or even danger. There is no denying that you will learn from the situation (probably retrospectively) but there is also no other *expert* to call on that will tell you what to do. You are on your own. You need to be able to constantly adapt and re-interpret whatever you have previously learned as new situations emerge. It is also an occasion when time spent ensuring that systems and processes are fully operational, well-practiced and robust add to the resilience of the whole operation and make the experience tolerable.

And it is this ability to *navigate* (Wood, 2017) or *knowing as we go* (Ingold, 2000) that I believe the process of entrepreneurial learning in teams offers us. The exciting concept for me is that it's already out there – our mission (should we decide to accept it) – is to embrace the role of the Team Coach as a fellow learners and curators of The Process. The *guide at the side* rather than the *sage on the stage* – or as one of my team entrepreneur students said, *the ghost in the room*, which I take as a compliment.

The Team Academy concept currently exists predominantly (but not exclusively) in the arena of higher education business qualifications. In his insightful video address recorded for the 25th celebration gathering of Tiimiakatemia held in Jyvaskyla, Finland, 2018, Peter Senge[1] likened traditional business schools to factories whose output was an MBA with questionable competencies. He complimented TA by explaining how their students may reach the same goal, but equipped with the necessary skills and attributes to be more effective actors

Perhaps it is time for a new paradigm for entrepreneurship; a relevant definition and proper understanding of *teams* and *teaming*; a critical evaluation of education; and a better vision of *future fit* learning.

Perhaps TA is indeed an idea whose time has come.

Note

1. Peter Senge's video address is available online at https://youtu.be/2BBEiTFqw7c

References

Ingold, T. (2000). *The perception of the environment: Essays in livelihood, dwelling and skill.* Routledge.

Nonaka, I., & Takeuchi, H. (1995). *The knowledge-creation company: How Japanese companies create the dynamics of innovation.* Oxford University Press.

Wood, P. (2017). Holiploigy, navigating the complexity of teaching in higher education. *Journal of Learning Development in Higher Education, 11.*

Concluding Thoughts

Contributors' Conversation

Elinor Vettraino and Berrbizne Urzelai

Throughout this book, you will have met a number of researchers, practitioners and learners all working with the Team Academy (TA) model and philosophy of entrepreneurial team learning. What follows is an amalgamation of a number of conversations that have taken place over the development of this book, along with responses to some core questions about the place and purpose of the TA model in entrepreneurship education. To help focus the thinking about the model, we invited authors to consider responses to questions around the challenges faced when creating TA programmes, the key learning that has come out of engaging with the TA model, and what the future of TA might be post COVID-19. The emerging conversations that follow offer some indication of some of the contributors' thoughts about the model and approach.

ELINOR VETTRAINO: I want to start with something that relates to the challenges of the TA model and that is actually something that you said, Col, in your book *How to teach entrepreneurship*. You said that it takes a lot of courage to teach entrepreneurship education (EE) in a way that is authentic for you, the deliverer (Jones, 2019). I wondered if you could say a bit about that in this context.

COLIN JONES: Sure. A lot of the focus for entrepreneurship educators has been on the first *E*, the entrepreneurship bit, and not so much on the *educator* bit. How do we as deliverers of learning, learn? How do we teach others how to learn? Thinking about this *educator* element, one of the biggest challenges will be about how we slow down education enough to enable learners to truly engage in the reflective element that is required to make sense of experiences. Getting institutions to understand that real learning matters when preparing students for the unknown is crucial to helping them function outside of an academic setting.

DOI: 10.4324/9781003163091-10

ALISON FLETCHER: As someone from outside academia, I've been disappointed by the lack of appreciation of practice-based education and the fact that, while some universities appear to pay lip-service to the idea of a Teaching Excellence Framework,[1] this appears to be more of a compliance exercise rather than a genuine attempt to improve the quality of the educational experience.

CHRIS JACKSON: I would agree with both of you, Alison and Col. The biggest challenge here has to be support or *buy-in* from the organization hosting the course. TA courses are perceived by some to be *resource intensive* and that doesn't always sit well with those in institutions that don't understand the model or processes involved.

SOPHIA KOUSTAS: I think from our observations and experiences, organizations share common challenges in creating TA-based programmes and these do include things like curriculum design, funding, and securing spaces.

ISAAC AMOAKO: Certainly, ensuring that the experiential learning ethos is achieved while meeting the traditional HE requirements for embedding theory into teaching and learning is definitely a challenge in curriculum design and delivery.

CHRIS: Yes, I think a clear commitment to support which includes dedicated learning spaces, as well as staff development, future growth and also how to sell and market the programme, all need to be established and supported at a senior level.

SUE LOSAPIO: I would agree, Chris. Leadership support and being able to navigate the bureaucracy in organizations is key. I like what you said about supporting staff development as well, and really helping those involved with the process of unlearning how to *teach*. I think that the coaching training and being in a supportive environment for that is so important.

ELINOR: Yes, unlearning is a really tricky beast! And one I am definitely still practicing.

COLIN: I don't think you're alone there. I don't think it's just about the educators changing their understanding. I think another challenge is getting enough students to want to become introspective. To slow down and become interested in the lives of others, the others in their team and their community. How do we help them to do that and to understand that it will advance their own lives?

CHRIS: I think there's also a challenge relating to how coached learning is seen. It feels as though it is somehow seen as not *real* or *robust* and that can lead to skepticism from colleagues who don't share a vision of wider models of learning and assessment.

ISAAC: Yes, not just colleagues but also getting leaders in HE to accept the *unconventional* TA model at all is a challenge. A radical mindset and approach to EE is required and we as authors here can be the champions and advocates for this approach.

ALISON: I think that is very true, and I agree that it is important for our community to work together to shape opinion and shift mindsets, both within the profession and in educational policy.

CHRIS: I agree. I think the way to counter these challenges is through publicity and openly engaging and communicating with the world, similar to the way in which organizations like EEUK have engaged with establishments in promoting the embedding of enterprise and entrepreneurship into the curriculum; perhaps there's a conversation to be had there?

BERRBIZNE URZELAI: Good point. Thinking about the key learning that we have had as implementers, or supporters, of this model, I have been affected by how much this has changed my view of my role as an educator. I'm curious about what you have noticed as core learning with this approach.

SOPHIA: For me the learning is around the process of developing the programme. This approach is best developed as a niche programme rather than as a mixed model, I think.

SUE: Yes, I would agree. And also, the importance of remembering that successful implementation of this programme is just like starting a business; it takes three times the time, three times the money, and three times the effort that you think it will!

SOPHIA: True but it's great to be part of such an incredible international network.

BERRBIZNE: Yes, international links are really important. And understanding how to operate in different teams is part of that too.

ALISON: Yes indeed. Team-working has to be learned; it doesn't *just happen*. And I think that also relates to the fact that coaching is not a solo sport. Coaches who operate in team coaching processes have to be coaching in teams.

CHRIS: It's certainly not easy! It can be challenging but very rewarding. I think it's also important to say that it works but it's not for every learner.

ALISON: True, and I wonder if that is also about lack of self-belief, fear of failure and a reticence to dream big which I think are all holding back our young people.

COLIN: I have been reminded that entrepreneurship happens when you are on your way to somewhere else! Team Academy is a neat way of getting students to *go somewhere else*. As such, it shows us that the pathways to effective learning are always unpredictable and not always managed neatly from one week to the next.

ISAAC: I agree, and also that is what makes the TA model relevant for students of EE given that entrepreneurship as a process requires experience which undoubtedly is subjective, and context based. That is also a challenge because it cannot be achieved in the traditional classroom. Marrying the two approaches is complex and very challenging to implement. However, TA is more effective at training enterprising and entrepreneurial students and there is a real need to do this now more than ever before because of the huge numbers of people who will be laid off globally following COVID.

ELINOR: A great point to make Isaac, and one that leads on to the question about post COVID TA; what do you see as the future of post COVID TA based learning?

SUE: Definitely, TA-based learning during COVID provided many opportunities to continuously reconnect and renew faith in trusting the process! The pandemic has fostered a sense of community within the team learning network by capitalizing on existing knowledge and welcoming new perspectives.

SOPHIA: I think post-COVID opportunities will exist in continuously iterating best practices, broadening the network, implementing the pedagogy into other disciplines such as engineering, education, and fostering innovation.

COLIN: I'd agree. I am hopeful that post-COVID19, education will slow down sufficiently to enable the Team Academy approach to become better synced with mainstream education offerings. I also think that this will be more likely if learning becomes more localized, less travel for the sake of travel, because Team Academy makes it possible to develop an uncommon interest in the common place, and to do so in the virtual world.

ALISON: I certainly think that operating in the virtual world will become more commonplace. Blended learning will become the norm which will enable collaboration both around the UK and internationally, and I can see us taking elements of the methodology into a much wider range of environments, from other academic programmes to extra-curricular, community and volunteering activities.

ISAAC: Yes, COVID has shown the importance of virtual teaching and learning so moving forward the TA model needs to consider incorporating elements of virtual teaching and learning such as virtual business trips and simulations, in the curricula.

ELINOR: Chris? The final thought to you on this.

CHRIS: It is probable that developing an entrepreneurial mindset and approach to learning is very appropriate in a VUCA world, and this has been emphasized with the COVID pandemic. I think history would suggest that as we emerge from COVID there will be an upsurge in an interest in enterprise generation and that the UK Government will want to support this. Being able to offer programmes that can equip our young, and perhaps *not-so-young*, people to be *mission ready* upon graduation – equipped with future-fit learning capabilities and agile in international networks – should position them as attractive action-learning packages. Seems like a win-win to me!

As is quite often the case, at the end of our discussions in this book, the first of the series, we were left with more questions to consider about the future of TA in the broader context of entrepreneurial activity. Rather than being the end of the story, this is very much the beginning. Book 2: *Team Academy in Practice* takes the journey forward into what TA is in practice, exploring research and narratives from those in the field who are working with and developing academic TA-based programmes of study. Book 3: *Team Academy: Leadership and Teams* considers how leadership and the concept of teams emerge and are defined in the TA model. And the final book, Book 4: *Team Academy in Diverse Settings*, considers TA as it appears outside of traditional TA based settings, considering how TA might work in industry, schools, communities of practice and beyond, and the legacy that it has left in learners and practitioners. There are many more stories to be told, and certainly more research to be done into this emergent model. Join us to further the conversation!

Note

1. The Teaching Excellence Framework (TEF) was introduced by the UK Government in 2016 as a metric to assess excellence in relating to teaching in higher education (HE). There are three levels, Gold, Silver and Bronze, with Gold standard being the highest awarded to HE institutions.

References

Jones, C. (2019). *How to teach entrepreneurship*. Edward Elgar.

Index

Note: Page numbers in italics indicate a figure and page numbers in bold indicate a table on the corresponding page.

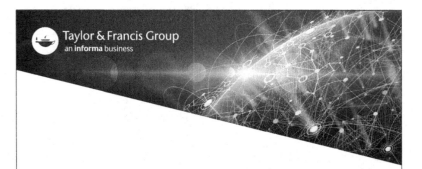

Printed in the United States
by Baker & Taylor Publisher Services